Experiential Learning in Higher Education:
Linking Classroom and Community

by Jeffrey A. Cantor

ASHE-ERIC Higher Education Report No. 7, 1.

Prepared by

Clearinghouse on Higher Education
The George Washington University

In cooperation with

Association for the Study
of Higher Education

Published by

Graduate School of Education and Human Development
The George Washington University

Jonathan D. Fife, Series Editor

1995. *Experiential Learning in Higher
g Classroom and Community.* ASHE-ERIC
Higher Education Report No. 7. Washington, D.C.: The
George Washington University, Graduate School of
Education and Human Development.

Library of Congress Catalog Card Number 96-79653
ISSN 0884-0040
ISBN 1-878380-71-0

Managing Editor: Lynne J. Scott
Manuscript Editor: Alexandra Rockey
Cover Design by Michael David Brown, Rockville, Maryland

Publication Date: 1997

The ERIC Clearinghouse on Higher Education invites individuals to submit proposals for writing monographs for the
ASHE-ERIC Higher Education Report series. Proposals must
include:
1. A detailed manuscript proposal of not more than five
   pages.
2. A chapter-by-chapter outline.
3. A 75-word summary to be used by several review committees for the initial screening and rating of each proposal.
4. A vita and a writing sample.

ERIC Clearinghouse on Higher Education
Graduate School of Education and Human Development
The George Washington University
One Dupont Circle, Suite 630
Washington, DC 20036-1183

This publication was prepared partially with funding from
the Office of Education Research and Improvement, U.S.
Department of Education, under contract no. ED RR-93-
002008. The opinions expressed in this report do not neces-
sarily reflect the positions or policies of OERI or the
Department.

EXECUTIVE SUMMARY

This review of the literature focuses on experiential learning in higher education. This review is, in fact, timely, as there is renewed academic interest in experiential learning. While the literature suggests that experiential learning is a necessary and vital component of formal instruction in colleges and universities, controversy nevertheless exists among scholars and educators about its place and use. These issues include:

A need for educated workers and citizens who can meet the challenges of a new world economy and order;
An increased understanding of learning theories and cognitive development;
More nontraditional learners with multitudes of learning styles and needs;
A changing American workplace which requires people to effectively interface with each other and understand their roles as team players;
An economic necessity for higher education to more closely interface with business and community; and
Administrative and faculty concerns about their roles in selection and control and evaluation of the learning process.

This review of the literature provides the academic community with an understanding of the current state-of-the-art practices in experiential learning, with suggestions for program design and development and operation.

Is Experiential Learning a Necessary and Appropriate Instructional Component of Higher Education?

The current literature suggests that experiential learning is a necessary component of formal instruction in colleges and universities for several reasons. First, faculty are concerned with optimizing the chances for their students to more easily enter their chosen professions or meet their desired goals upon graduation from the college program due to decreasing job markets and increasing competition among college graduates across most fields of study (CAEL 1990; Gettys 1990). Rosenbaum cites a mutual concern among teachers and employers about the effectiveness of preparing our future generations for the American workforce at all levels — technical and professional (1992).

Second, the typical college student is becoming more complex. More nontraditional learners are opting for college study and demanding more varied modes of learning (Kerka 1989). Also, student recruitment, retention, and completion rates are a major concern of most college faculty. Seibert, Hart, and Sypher (1989) and Baker et al. (1991) document the benefits of experiential learning for student career decisionmaking and development. Interestingly enough, students tend to continue their education into graduate schools at a significantly increased rate after participating in experiential learning as part of an undergraduate program, according to O'Neill (1992) and Gregory (1990).

In Which Programs Do We Find Experiential Learning Components?

Experiential learning as a formal part of college and university curricula extends across the range of subject areas and disciplines. As college faculty recognize a need to provide experiential learning opportunities into their courses and programs to make learning more relevant for their students, more and more literature is emerging, spanning the disciplines from the social-sciences programs to the arts and humanities. Hence, these programs exist across the broad spectrum of higher education today — including English literature, history, psychology, communications, etc., — not just in the terminal or occupational areas. Experiential learning activities include cooperative education placements, practicum experiences, and classroom-based hands-on laboratory activities. College educators find experiential learning a valuable adjunct to traditional instruction in these disciplines. The experiences outside of the classroom provide the increasingly growing numbers of nontraditional learners with valuable opportunities to apply theory to practice (Rolls 1992).

And What About the Professional and Technical Programs?

Disciplines in the professional and technical disciplines including education and the health careers and social work are using experiential learning instructional techniques to provide students with the competencies necessary to pursue successful careers upon graduation (Baxter Magolda 1993; Hightower 1993).

These experiences, in turn, allow learners to develop skills and amass job experience which gives them an edge on the competition for initial employment upon graduation. In many cases, the accreditation organizations supporting the disciplines have specific requirements for such experiential learning activities.

The need to provide college students with opportunities to reinforce social and ethical values has caused college faculty to consider ways to incorporate service-learning activities into the formal curriculum (Stanton 1988). Usually in the form of volunteer service, these activities allow students to apply classroom learning to real-world community needs and simultaneously serve their neighbors. Disciplines spanning the curriculum have used service-learning activities.

How Can We Link Classroom and Community for Economic Development Through Experiential Learning?

The literature reveals some not-so-obvious outcomes of experiential learning as well (Cantor 1990). Through development of cooperative education programs, colleges and their faculty and students are brought closer to their communities. Through these newly formed links, proactive economic development outcomes emerge. These include better educated and trained students as potential employees, technology transfer from faculty to entrepreneurs via business-development consultation, and the like.

Finally, through this review we will highlight, discuss, and describe the ways that faculty are using experiential learning activities, the issues surrounding their use, and faculty and administrative practices requisite to development and operation of such experiential learning activities. These include selling the concept within a faculty governance structure, developing program objectives, marketing the program to the community as well as to the student, administration of experiential learning activities, and program evaluation.

CONTENTS

FOREWORD

Recently, the ASHE-ERIC Higher Education Reports series published works by Kuh, Douglas, Lind, and Ramin-Gyurnek called *Learning Outside the Classroom: Transcending Artificial Boundaries*. This report reviewed the conditions that foster a climate in which out-of-classroom experiences can contribute to greater educational productivity. In another recent report by Love and Goodsell Love, *Enhancing Student Learning: Intellectual, Social, and Emotional Integration*, the need to carefully integrate classroom cognitive development with out-of-classroom affective development was reviewed.

This report on experiential learning by Jeffrey A. Cantor, director of technical education at the Virginia Community College System in Richmond, is a further examination of the contributions that linking classroom and out-of-classroom formal educational experiences can have on a student's overall academic program.

Historically, experiential learning more often than not has been relegated to a few cooperative education programs. These programs, primarily based in the professional schools of engineering, business, and education, provided students with the opportunity to alternate formal classroom learning with on-the-job experiences. To a large extent, what was learned in the classroom was not systematically used during the work experience and vice versa. Today's use of experiential learning takes a much more integrative approach between classroom and out-of-classroom experiences and between the academic mission and the outcomes from experiential learning.

As Cantor reviews in detail, there are several major reasons for an increased interest in experiential learning, including:

An increased sensitivity to the responsibility of higher education to develop a strong relationship between classroom learning and realities of our global community;

A broadening of our understandings of learning theory, cognitive development, social development, and emotional development; and

The need to broaden teaching styles used by faculty to more effectively relate to the multiple learning styles of the older, nontraditional student.

An acknowledgment of the knowledge base and career skill needs are changing so rapidly in our society that it is

---

increasingly important to train students how to be self-learners. Significant to the overall reputation of an academic program or institution is the ability to forge a stronger link between academic programs and the employers of their students and community.

In this report, the author first examines the politics and policy issue of experiential learning and reviews the intellectual foundation of experiential programs of the arts and humanities and the social sciences, and technical and professional disciplines. The author concludes his report with a synthesis of successful experiential practices involved with designing experiential activities, assessing student needs, and evaluating these programs.

This report will help to develop an informed base of discussion as academic programs and institutions review their philosophy, mission, and practice concerning experiential learning. This report also can act as a reality check as institutions evaluate the effectiveness of their current experiential learning activities.

Jonathan D. Fife
Series Editor,
Professor of Higher Education Administration and
Director, ERIC Clearinghouse on Higher Education

ACKNOWLEDGMENTS

My thanks to Sandrea DeMinco and Susan Voge, librarians at Lehman College in New York City, for their efforts and expertise in identifying and securing much of the literature that ultimately formed the database of this report. Additionally, I wish to thank my wife, Ruth, for her tireless efforts in the preparation of this manuscript.

OVERVIEW: THE POLITICS AND POLICY ISSUES

This review of the literature focuses on experiential learning in higher education. The work is, in fact, timely, as we are witnessing a renewed academic interest in experiential learning as an instructional strategy in higher education. Certain themes and issues are prevalent throughout the literature on this topic. Among them, to meet the demands of society, learning must be dynamic, lifelong, and relevant to learner needs.

This report will discuss contemporary thought about how experiential education can catalytically serve to help higher education and its constituent communities form learning communities through cooperative linkages (Barnett and Bayne 1992). Furthermore, it is the author's intention to describe the current state-of-the-art practices in experiential learning across the curriculum in higher education. As a review of the literature, the ultimate goal is to provide suggestions for program improvement and/or design, development, and operation.

Definitions of Experiential Learning

Experiential learning has been discussed and described both as a process of learning and a method of instruction. Cross reminds us that experiential learning has been around since the beginning of time (1994[a]). Experiential education, on the other hand, has been discussed, described, and debated as "an alternative" and/or "an enrichment" to instruction, and "a philosophy!" Clements cites Stevens and Richards' (1992) definition: "Experiential education can be defined as immersing students in an activity (ideally, closely related to course material) and then asking for their reflection on the experience" (1995, p. 116). Experiential education refers to learning activities that engage the learner directly in the phenomena being studied. This learning can be in all types of work or service settings by undergraduate and graduate students of all ages (Kendall et al. 1986). Hence, as a method of education it facilitates active multisensory involvement of one's students in some aspect of the course content. This immersion in the material becomes the basis for analysis and reflection on the part of the student — and hence the learning.

Predominant Forms of Experiential Education

Higher education faculty are creative in their approaches to designing learning environments. Faculty in the arts and humanities have reported to facilitate learning through role plays in languages and literature, student-run radio stations in communications, and reenactments in history. In the social and behavioral sciences it is not uncommon to read reports of students working in community-based organizations and clinics in forms of service learning. In the physical sciences and mathematics areas students are reported to benefit from laboratories and manipulative experiences. And in the professional areas such as health and education, practicums and clinicals in health-care agencies and school-based fieldwork and internships are not uncommon.

Another prominent method of delivering experiential learning cooperatively with business and community is in a planned program of cooperative education. As such it deserves a formal definition. Cooperative education is defined as: " . . . the integration of classroom theory with practical work experience under which students have specific periods of attendance . . . and specific periods of employment" (Collings and Cohen 1977, p. 13 in Vickers 1990). Cooperative higher education is further explained by the National Commission for Cooperative Education (undated) as:

> . . . an academic strategy that integrates on-campus classroom study with off-campus work experience. Students in cooperative education programs alternate between periods of study in their colleges and universities and periods of employment in business, government, and nonprofit organizations. Employment areas are usually directly related to academic areas (p. i).

Thus cooperative education is an academically based experience for students, administered cooperatively by the educational institution, local business and industry, and the community at large.

At many liberal-arts colleges where experiential learning is used, it occurs via these classroom-based activities, such as cooperative education, internships, and other formal instructional activities, including volunteer service and student-exchange programs. In this report we will explore in detail use of these activities as instructional tools for potential enhancement of classroom learning, as well as the other innovative experientially based learning activities uncovered in the literature. This discussion will provide unique insights into the movement toward bridging academe and its various communities.

Current Levels of Participation in Experiential Education

Available data suggests that by 1990 more than 1,000 post-secondary institutions (community colleges, four-year colleges, and universities) have offered some form of experiential education, serving more than 250,000 students.

Heinemann and Wilson surveyed 20 institutions of higher education (18 senior colleges and two community colleges) to determine levels of participation in experiential learning (1995). They found that internships, practicums, and cooperative education programs were in place in 75 percent of the 205 programs reported. However, this study did not seek specific information about classroom-based experiential learning activities.

At this point, some analysis of cooperative education as but one method of experiential education, external to the classroom, is in order. According to Dube, colleges and universities " . . . were offering cooperative education as a means of meeting institutional missions, providing a more complete education for their students, and strengthening their institutions' academic and economic position" (1990, p. 771). About 45 percent of these are two-year colleges and the remainder are four-year and/or graduate institutions.

Students participate in cooperative education for many reasons. These include those financial benefits which help pay for their education, to the benefits to be derived in learning to perform in their chosen occupations or careers, and to experiences gained for job-placement purposes. Increasing numbers of faculty recognize the benefits of providing students with real-world experiences that complement formal classroom study.

Employers recognize the benefits of joining with the college to produce a better worker. They also gain from early evaluation of students as potential workers prior to making long-term employment commitments. Approximately 50,000 employers have participated in postsecondary cooperative education. Hoberman reports that larger employers such as IBM and General Motors account for only 4,000 of the

In the social and behavioral sciences it is not uncommon to read reports of students working in community-based organizations and clinics in forms of service learning.

approximately 250,000 college students enrolled in cooperative-education programs at a given time (1994). This fact is significant in terms of the economic-development benefits that can accrue to smaller employers and the community at large through participation in experiential education, as will be discussed later in this work.

A Conceptual Framework for Analyzing Current Practices

As faculty, why should we be concerned about the way in which we present our subject matter? Many faculty ask: Why change what works and has worked through the ages? This is but some of the rhetoric one hears in promoting experiential learning activities for our students. Heinemann and Wilson offer:

> *Critics contend that college teaching today is essentially the same as it has been in the past. Most faculty rely upon a didactic approach to instruction. Students are often viewed as "empty vessels" with professors having the responsibility of pouring in knowledge from the discipline* (1995, p 46).

However, as faculty including Matson and Matson have discovered, "Students are demanding relevance in their educations, especially within the liberal arts" (1995, p. 13). The world is becoming more complex, more technological, and more competitive. Therefore, one issue emanating from the literature is:

- A need for educated workers and citizens who can meet the challenges of a new world economy and order.

Cross describes the current interest in experiential learning in terms of contemporary forces or pressures within our social and educational environments (1994[a]). She argues that there is an urgent need in society for well-educated workers and citizens who can effectively apply their acquired knowledge to meet real-world problems. These real-world problems are brought about by a new economy and increased world competition, Cross further argues, which requires that students as workers and citizens be able to interpret trends, exercise sound judgment, and display personal initiative to succeed and compete.

Laws, Rosborough, and Poodry (1995) concur with Cross. They add the fact that the constructivist nature of an activity-based curricula facilitates the development of scientific reasoning and conceptual model-building abilities in students which, in turn, results in refinement of those reasoning and judgment abilities Cross views as essential. The means by which this occurs is explained by Catelli, who quotes Sirotnik as stating:

> . . . inquiry is to be made 'critical' by the participants of the partnership engaging in rigorous questioning and then conducting constructive dialogue as they examine descriptive data and compare it to existing knowledge, their programmatic values, and their practical wisdom and experience. The heart of the inquiry resides not only in being critical, but in being collaborative and directed at action . . . (1995, p. 28).

Cross adds:

> . . . the greatest demand on education for the future will be to prepare students to think, to solve problems, to apply knowledge, to engage in constructive teamwork, and most important of all, perhaps, to develop their capacity to continue to learn throughout their lives (p. 22).

Yes, it is possible to maintain academic integrity and yet build a climate in which students can experience the body of knowledge and skills within a discipline, in an active and collaborative manner, wherein they are challenged to master and learn, and where they also have an opportunity to gain those reasoning, decisionmaking, cultural, social, and leadership skills so badly needed in today's and tomorrow's societies.

To design educational programs that best meet learner goals, another issue that surfaces is:

- An increased understanding of learning theories and cognitive development.

The genesis of experiential education as an educational process often is credited to John Dewey's constructs of experiential learning. Dewey's view was:

> *Education at coop institutions will have to encompass two overreaching goals: 1) integration of classroom and workplace learning, and 2) education that will provide students with the tools to transform the workplace into an environment that fosters complete self-realization* (Saltmarsh 1992, p. 9).

Parnell, an advocate for contextual learning, senses a dichotomy between what is demonstrated to be sound instructional practices and what all too often is happening in the classroom, as he offers, "What we do in much of contemporary pedagogy is require students to commit bits of knowledge to memory in isolation from any practical application and to simply take our word that they 'might need it someday'" (1996, p. 18).

As such, students will not see requisite meaning in the content and fall short of mastery for future use and problem-solving. He argues for a match between what has been demonstrated in the field of human cognition and what educators practice in the classroom, and elaborates:

> *Psychologists, philosophers, and educators from William James to Jerome Bruner to Howard Gardner have made the case for making connections in education. In the last few decades, brain research has shown that the need for developing connections is rooted in the basic function of the brain itself. When we teach for connectedness we are teaching in accordance with the way the human brain operates* (p. 19).

Perhaps the most powerful words spoken by Cross in the keynote address at the 22nd annual national conference of the National Society for Experiential Education were: "Research in cognitive psychology suggests that experiential education has built into it many pedagogical advantages that must be artificially created in academic education" (p. 22). A review of modern psychology in and of itself would suggest that educators take a close look at the: (1) importance of active vs. passive learning; and (2) the conception of the schema as the network of the mind that organizes and stores learning. Cross and other learning theorists view learning as transformational, rather than additive.

Moore (1990) discusses Kolb's Theory, which suggests that learning proceeds through a cycle, moving from concrete experience to reflective observation, to abstract conceptualization, and finally to active experimentation. Hence, this connectedness issue, as Parnell views it, " . . . runs through our educational institutions as well as through our communities and our world" (p. 18).

Cross elaborates: "New learning interacts with what we already know to transform and deepen our understanding" (1994[a], p. 23). This, she further elaborates, suggests that learning is active and dynamic — a process "in which connections are constantly changing and the structure reformatted" (p. 23). Further insights into the relationship between cognitive development and experiential learning is gained through Parnell's summation that:

> *Since the brain is a physiological organ, it seems reasonable to hypothesize that the physical structure of the brain can change as the result of experience and that an educational environment as rich in experience as in information can have a positive impact upon brain development and knowledge retention.*
>
> *Every time an individual experiences something that 'connects' with a previous experience, that experience will tend to 'stick,' and something will be learned* (p. 20).

Therefore, through this review we explore the issues and information available about the value of experiential learning activities as facilitators to learner cognitive development and learning mastery. However, we recognize that our classes are populated with diverse students with varying needs and interests. Hence, a change in demographics necessitates a review and analysis of learner needs and best learning styles. An issue to be addressed by this review of the literature is to determine how appropriate and valuable experiential learning's as an instructional tool to meet the needs of a changing student population. The third issue to be addressed is:

Experiential learning activities are natural motivators. We know that adult learners need to get involved in and take ownership for their own learning.

- More nontraditional learners with multitudes of learning styles and needs.

The demographics of our student population in colleges across the country has changed to more closely reflect the changing American population. Increasingly more students are not native English speakers, and more represent ethnic, racial, and gender minorities. Many also are single parents and principal breadwinners with a need to financially support their families — something often afforded to students through internship and clinical experiences.

With an increase in the numbers of nontraditional learners comes a proportionate increase in the numbers of older learners — average age late 20s to early 30s — absent from the classroom for a long time; as well as students who have physical limitations; and those learners who have a long personal history of academic failure and a need to build self-confidence.

How effectively do we match instruction to our learner populations? Motivation is the key to learning. Parnell insists:

> *For teaching to be truly effective, the student must be motivated to connect the content of knowledge with the context of application, thus utilizing the ability of the thinking brain to solve problems and to assimilate that knowledge in a way that can be useful in new situations. Learning should utilize the brain's large cerebrum computer capacity to make the connections between content and context, academic and technical* (p. 20).

Experiential learning activities are natural motivators. We know that adult learners need to get involved in and take ownership for their own learning (Cantor 1992[a]). When learners understand the value of a certain knowledge or skill and are correspondingly excited about it, learning can take place. Students are motivated to learn by becoming more involved in the learning experience, thus linking theory to practice.

Cognitive psychology addresses the need for learners to be ready to learn before learning can take place. We call this the "teachable moment" (Cantor 1992[a]). Both Baslow and Byrne (1993) and Gregory (1990) have cited rationale and research findings to support the motivational benefits to learners by active and participative learning. Experiential learning has proved to be such an effective technique that promotes a learner's cognitive development (Mosser 1989; Acosta 1991; Zeuschner 1991).

And with an increasing number of learners with either learning and/or physical difficulties entering the mainstream college classroom, many of our students also need the multi-sensory reinforcement which results from structured "hands-on" learning. Multiple sensory involvement via structured work activities has been proved highly successful (Saltmarsh 1992). Bolstered self-confidence is important to all learners but especially to nontraditional learners (Mosier 1990). Seibert and Davenport-Sypher (1989) suggest that college retention rates of learners improved as a result of involvement in experiential learning. This is a significant reason for its instructional use in the college classroom.

Polirstok sees a direct connection between learning environment and student cultural experiences. She offers: " . . . understanding the cultural diversity-learning connection raises many questions for instructors in terms of their teaching practices" (1996, p. 2). As more nontraditional learners (e.g., older, second-career, minority, or disadvantaged) are opting for college study, they are demanding more varied modes of learning (Kerka 1989). Many bring other "cognitive" or learning difficulties to the classroom. Laws, Rosborough, and Poodry raise the gender issue as well. They see experiential learning mitigating the problem of recruiting females into jobs traditionally held by males in the physical sciences. An activity-based curriculum can help close the gender gap, they contend.

The mature student oftentimes is pressured by time conflicts — work and family. This student needs to see a direct relevance of course content to one's needs. Experiential learning is personalized and thus this unique characteristic can effectively complement traditional classroom experiences for adults as learners by providing an opportunity for reinforcement of learning through individual clarification and practice.

When learners understand the value of a certain knowledge or skill and are correspondingly excited about it, learning can take place.

Also, student recruitment, retention, and completion rates are a major concern of most college faculty. Seibert and Davenport-Sypher (1989) and Baker-Loges and Duckworth (1991) document the benefits of experiential learning for student career decisionmaking and for career development. These experiences, which often occur outside of the classroom, provide the increasingly growing numbers of nontraditional as well as traditional learners with valuable opportunities to apply theory to practice (Rolls 1992). These experiences in turn allow all learners to develop skills and amass job experience which gives them an edge on the competition for initial employment upon graduation. Interestingly enough, students tend to continue their education into graduate school at a significantly increased rate after participating in experiential learning as part of an undergraduate program, according to O'Neill (1992) and Gregory (1990).

Our American workplace is a microcosm of American society. Coupled with that is a changing work organization requiring more team effort and social skills. Our educational institutions must provide opportunities for students to develop these skills along with their other studies. Therefore, the next issue behind the experiential learning movement is:

- A changing American workplace that requires people to effectively interface with each other and understand their roles as team players.

Moore discusses the changing images of work and of the workplace and their impact on college-level instruction and instructional practices (1994[a]). Economic and organizational shifts caused in part by globalization of business, rapid technological developments, and increasing demands for quality in goods and services are affecting corresponding changes in the workplace, necessitating increased reliance on work teams, worker flexibility, and worker decisionmaking. All of these factors have placed pressures on entrepreneurs and managers to ensure quality in their workforces — hence our students. Inherent in these workplace changes will be a need for workers at all levels to be continuous learners.

How we provide learning opportunities for our students to gain the skills and knowledge to effectively interact with one another in a teamwork environment often is a troublesome task. We have developed an educational culture that emphasizes competitiveness among students — for entrance into the university, for scholarships, for graduate school, for honors, etc. It is no wonder that upon graduation, students as workers and citizens have difficulty getting along! Yet, we realize that the changing American workplace requires effective interpersonal skills and teamwork (Moore 1994[b]).

One experiential learning activity the literature reveals as having been successful in this endeavor is service learning. Community service as a formal part of education, including higher education, quickly is becoming a national movement. From former President Bush's "Thousand Points of Light" to President Clinton's National Service Corps, federal initiatives recognize universal service as a means by which to better educate our youth. Academic programs of all kinds have capitalized upon the opportunities for service learning to become an integral part of college curricula. Service learning traditionally is viewed as a particular form of experiential learning, one that emphasizes for students the accomplishment of tasks that meet human needs in combination with conscious education growth (Stanton 1988).

Other types of experiential learning as well have proved successful in getting learners into an environment in which they must interact with one another and the community to apply their knowledge and skills in a given discipline. Lurie and Overbo applied the process to an evaluation research course (1995). They offer: "Working in the field enables students to experience the problems and opportunities of communicating and negotiating with stakeholders in the evaluation process. Students can be exposed to . . . often incompatible modes of thinking" (p. 253). In this report we explore the literature in service learning within college programs across the curriculum. Therefore, an important issue posed for this review of the literature is to analyze the potential of service learning as a viable mechanism for promoting experiential learning.

The aggregate of the above issues suggests a need for higher education institutions and their constituencies to move closer together to forge partnerships for learning communities — hence, the next issue.

• An economic necessity for higher education to more closely interface with business and community.

In her address, Cross offered the following comment which causes us to think about the relationship between the institution of higher education and its business and community neighbors. She asks: "Might it be possible to increase learning and lower costs through cooperation with other educational agencies in the society?" (p. 22). I read "other educational agencies in the society" to include all business and community institutions — which are necessary ingredients for the development of learning societies within business and community. Therefore, we must determine if experiential learning is a useful instructional tool for establishing a quid pro quo between higher education and business and community.

First, let's look at changes in the workplace. Moore identified several profound implications of a changing workplace for experiential educators (1994[b]). Among these were:

Competitiveness. He described the best-run firms' competitive success as emanating from application of several basic principles: a bias for action; closeness to customer; autonomy; entrepreneurship; productivity through people; lean staffing; and dedication to corporate values. To effect these, he continued, employees must fully participate in corporate decisionmaking, be autonomous in carrying out work, and be a full stakeholder in the firm's success. This happens only with the aid of continuous learning!

Teamwork. Moore notes that teamwork calls for a change in the nature of peer relationships. Likewise, a change is indicated in the practices of personnel supervision and evaluation and its distribution of power on the part of the organization.

Participatory Design. A significant implication of the new organization, according to Moore, will be in its reorganization of work practices. The essence of this new configuration is in the involvement of the worker in the management of work flow and the organization — hence an empowerment of workers.

Spiritual Growth. The message here is managing for dignity, meaning, and community. Total-quality relationships are necessary: trust, affection, and caring.

Democracy. In workplace democratization, workers will have more control over the working conditions, practices, and an equitable share of the profits as well. The workplace will become a rich learning environment. Moore quotes Wirth (1983):

> . . . *a democratic workplace . . . enhances the quality of people's opportunity for learning. An actively involved, thinking worker learns as he or she cooperates with his or her colleagues in making crucial decisions about the social and economic organization of the enterprise* (1994[b], p. 7).

The Learning Organization. Moore indicates that the modern organization for both economic and social reasons will need to "promote learning among its members, and learn itself as a collective entity." Practices that promote learning by individuals and groups — learning organizations — produce more effective outcomes. How then, can such organizations be created?

A Quid Pro Quo

The need for partnerships of business and education has reached the forefront of concern among educators and entrepreneurs alike (Mosser and Muller 1990). Moore's remarks are crucial to successful joint ventures with the university's community at large. Experiential education can be a catalyst for college — business and industry and community educational partnerships. But why are such partnerships of any interest to an academic?

First, promoting experiential learning partnerships with business and the community helps to maximize mutual resources. Mosier cites several reasons why partnerships are a necessary part of a college's mission, including: (1) its value as an entre to expanding scientific and research partnerships between university and business and industry; (2) its usefulness as a base for fund-raising development; and (3) the "learn and earn" opportunities provided for students needing additional financial support while pursuing higher education (1990). And the value of such partnerships also can be seen in the gaining of access to state-of-the-art facilities as documented by Kerka (1989). In many program disciplines, access to industry loaned or shared facilities makes the difference between operating programs or closing down admissions. The other side of the quid pro quo is in the access to faculty expertise and students-as-employees on the part of business and community.

Yes, faculty are concerned with optimizing the chances for their students to more easily enter their chosen professions or meet their desired goals upon graduation from the college program. This concern is exacerbated by decreasing job markets and increasing competition among college graduates across most fields of study (Gettys 1990). The literature documents that a significant relationship exists between students who have experiential learning, especially internship, clinical, and cooperative education experiences as part of a program of higher education and those who quickly secure jobs after completing the college program (Vickers 1990). Internships, practicums, clinicals, and cooperative education lead to a better opportunity for employment in one's chosen field upon graduation (Gettys 1990). Therefore the argument for a better understanding of experiential learning through cooperative education, internships, and practicum experiences also extends to the student as a new graduate. Furthermore, research indicates that students who participate in these forms of experiential education command higher starting salaries (Vickers 1990; Gettys 1990).

Finally, experiential learning partnerships also can provide better learning environments for adults and nontraditional students. In fact, Cayan and Jacquart cite additional benefits which are afforded the professor in one's efforts to expand the curriculum outside of the classroom — including a "helping hand" from businesspeople in the instructional process — both off and on campus — and a fresh perspective on the subject and state-of-the-art practices for the professor (1990). But the literature reveals considerable concerns on the part of faculty and administration about experiential learning in academe. Hence, the next issue.

- Faculty and administrative concerns about their roles in selection and control and evaluation of the learning process.

"Probably the greatest barrier to brain-based contextual teaching is the pressure to 'cover the material' mindset" (Parnell 1996). Sit in on any curriculum committee meeting where experiential learning activities are included on a course-development or course-change proposal, and one quickly learns about the politics of this issue. What are some of the predominant issues?

Issues addressed in this review of the literature include: existence of uniform collegewide administrative procedures to promote experiential learning activities across the curriculum; awarding of credit for experiential learning activities; student qualifications for participation in internships, clinicals, and cooperative education programs; curriculum decisionmaking prerogatives for experiential learning activities; and identification of the real college cost to operate experiential education programs (e.g., cooperative education, practicums, internships, and clinicals), including costs of faculty participation.

Factors that complicate use and institutionalization of experiential learning activities into the curriculum, according to Wagner, Scharinger, and Sisak (1995) and Wagner et al. (1992) are: (1) a growing demand for faculty to be both productive researchers and quality teachers; (2) larger class sizes; (3) a need for cultural-diversity training for faculty and staff; and (4) budget restrictions.

While significant numbers of faculty report the benefits of experiential learning as an embellishment for students' conceptual understanding and learning within the academic classroom, according to Feeney and Morris, formal experiential education may be shunned by some faculty as "contrary to or detracting from rigorous study in the academic disciplines" (1994, p. 14). They further offer that the content and methods of the particular academic disciplines, not the pedagogical practices, tend to define faculty interests at liberal-arts colleges with highly competitive admissions practices. Wagner's conclusions are that " . . . it is not the process of experiential training which has produced such dramatic results, rather it is how that process is integrated with program objectives that will determine the effectiveness of the program" (p. 4).

Yes, faculty are concerned with optimizing the chances for their students to more easily enter their chosen professions or meet their desired goals upon graduation from the college program. This concern is exacerbated by decreasing job markets and increasing competition among college graduates across most fields of study.

Administrative Issues and Concerns

The literature suggests that an issue for consideration is a need for uniform administrative procedures governing experiential learning (especially cooperative education and other external experiential education activities) (Muller 1989). Successful programs are those guided by well-thought-out policies and guidelines for student recruitment, screening, and placement. Another issue is academic justification for awarding credit for a student's workplace activity even as it relates to one's academic pursuits (Stoner 1989; Beales 1993; Parker and Keeling 1990).

Stoner also cites the issue of commonly used eligibility requirements for entrance into internship programs. A common policy requires upper-level class standing (junior or senior in four-year institutions; fourth semester in two-year programs) and a grade point average of 3.0 or better and possibly a 3.5 in the major. Siebert and Davenport-Sypher's work identified internship programs as restricted to majors with GPAs of 3.0 or better in 51 percent of those programs reviewed (1989). Clearly some faculty want only the best students in such programs.

Marketing of experiential education programs to minority or nontraditional student populations also is an issue (and oftentimes an added expense), as cited by Parker and Keeling (1990) and Mosser and Rea (1990). The nontraditional student population often is the same population who historically has had the most difficulty entering the workforce — even after amply preparing for job entry. Yet by maintaining the current practice of admitting only the most senior and best academic students to cooperative education opportunities, are we not perpetuating this barrier to our nontraditional student populations?

Other issues needing resolution include the process by which curriculum decisions are made respective to experiential learning — including central vs. departmental (or program control) of these programs; processes for credit for nondegree work and credit for nontraditional learning (for example, prior experience — and/or amounts of credit allowable for cooperative education within a degree program).

Experiential education programs cost money to operate. Often the real costs of these programs go unnoticed due to the increased burdens carried by faculty in an attempt to deliver the kinds of educational experiences they fully realize their students need to succeed academically and in their chosen careers. Muller discusses the cost of supervising students off-campus or at the work site and the necessary networking on the part of faculty within the business and industry community to foster cooperative relationships (1989).

Faculty compensation for internship supervision also has been a major administrative issue on the campus. The missing link to successful cooperative education often is a systematic campuswide scheme for compensating faculty, according to Muller.

And finally, Cross' concerns about evaluation of experiential learning need to be addressed (1989[b]). Certainly different procedures need to be used to evaluate experiential learning, whether in the classroom setting or in the field. How faculty interface with others, the field preceptors, or on-the-job supervisors of students, etc., needs to be analyzed and discussed.

In Summary

What this author wishes to convey through this review of the literature is a need for learning communities to be forged through partnerships between higher education and business and community. Perhaps the message is best conveyed in the words of Parnell, who states: The need for connectedness in education goes even deeper than the pressures of contemporary society or the demands of the workplace. The process of brain-based learning calls for making connections. And he cautions, "Unless connections are made between subject content and the context of application, little long-lasting learning occurs for the majority of students" (p. 19).

THE PROGRAMS — ARTS AND HUMANITIES AND THE SOCIAL SCIENCES

Experiential learning instructional pedagogy and the liberal arts — are these mutually exclusive entities? Academicians such as Stanton would say not (1990[a]). According to Thorburn, "Experiential learning is incompatible with more traditional learning only if the academy is incompatible with the society of which it is a part" (1990, p. 293). Very powerful words indeed!

Liberal-arts educators appear to be searching for active educational experiences for their students — those kinds of pedagogical activities which will " . . . enable and require them to reflect critically on the world around them — to link theory to practice and to induce, synthesize, and experiment with new knowledge" (Stanton 1990[a], p. 183).

A Point of Commencement
Let's look at the prominent issues identified from a liberal-arts disciplinary perspective.

Meeting the Challenges of a New World Economy and Order
The preceding section spoke to a changing world order and its impact upon the educational needs of its citizens and workers. The quandary, in terms of liberal-arts curricula, is how these programs of study can address the needs of citizens of a new world order. To begin, let's review the goals of a liberal-arts education. Mosser (1989) discusses these goals as to develop within a student:

communications skills
critical-thinking skills
interpersonal loyalty and intimacy
empathy, tolerance, and respect for others
a sense of self in a society, and a historical context
a cultural sophistication; and to
prepare for life's work
learn how to continually learn throughout life
clarify personal values and integrity

Are we as a community of intellectuals and educators helping our students to meet these goals in a traditional college classroom? Too many in our ranks say nay. O'Neil highlights

the state of the college classroom today by reflecting on
traditional liberal education in the United States, circa 1850.

> *The academic programs of the colleges in the first half
> of the 19th century were amazingly uniform in their
> structure and content. . . . There was, as well, a shared
> and unified sense about the moral order of the uni-
> verse. . . . This sort of undergraduate education was
> possible for several important reasons. First, the social
> world of the first half of the 19th century was a homo-
> geneous one for most Americans. Most of the citizens of
> the country were natives of or descendants of natives of
> the British Isles . . . were by-and-large Protestants from
> other northern European countries. . . . Intellectually,
> socially, economically, and politically the nonnative
> inhabitants of the new nation shared a heritage with
> each other* (1990, p. 191).

A very easy world in which to educate youth indeed it was.
But alas, this no longer is the case. Our world today, as
already has been discussed, is far more complicated. To
liberally educate today, new pedagogy must be identified or
developed.

What more must today's liberal-arts student be able to do?
We spoke at length about the characteristics necessary for
success moving toward the next century. Stanton adds to
this discourse by citing Locker (1986) who insisted that:
"Unless one carries knowledge into acts of application, generalization, and experimentation, one's learning is incomplete." Stanton, among others, sees a need to find a
pedagogy that is more active and involving — enabling the
learner to take responsibility for one's learning. Stanton
offers: "In the area of content, we have failed to educate
students effectively with both an understanding of the social
issues and an awareness of the traditional responsibilities of
democratic citizenship" (p. 179). He argues that we cannot
continue to view civic education separate from content
using the excuse that civic education lacks academic sub-
stance. And Greenberg adds: "There is probably no more
central concept, no better idea in the discourse on college-
level educational improvement, than the concept of active
learning" (1995, p. 4).

Taylor et al. discuss the intrinsic value of experiential

learning in higher education (1994). Emphasis is primarily aimed at relating classroom theory to the real world. This especially is needed in the broad liberal arts, as many of our students in core curriculum classrooms take such courses as a necessary part of their respective majors and not because they particularly desire or appreciate the value of such learning. For these students, Taylor et al. indicates how coordinated work experiences make classwork more realistic and relevant for the student. This realism, in turn, creates increased motivation for more intense academic work. And as faculty, we should be concerned about creating an active, thus positive, learning atmosphere for our students.

There are several key ingredients necessary to construct effective active-learning strategies, as Greenberg offers. Among them is "critical thinking." This renewed emphasis on critical thinking is what causes traditional professors the greatest problem. Herein, faculty must accomplish much more in terms of their students' cognitive development to apply learning to new situations, answer complex questions, and use central concepts, all with fewer resources. Effective assessment techniques must be in place to determine a match between a student's ability level and the material presented. The active teacher, interested in student learning which emphasizes the ability to think and solve complex problems, will change from a "dispenser of information" to a teacher whose primary role is in structuring complex academic tasks. To accomplish this monumental task, students must do the work to make them think critically and analytically about the content.

Greenberg discusses a second of his main ingredients, "context," as the degree to which the mission, reward structure, and institutional foundation supports faculty in their quest to become active teachers. He argues, " . . . if the context for teaching reflects a consistent valuing and support from campus and departmental level leadership, the potential for change is helped immeasurably" (p. 4).

Many of Mosser's goals should be necessary parts of all college liberal-arts programs, as Weinmann stresses (1992). College curriculum committees should take note. These goals should be supported through experiential learning experiences. Certainly faculty across the liberal arts, the arts and humanities, and social-sciences disciplines have seen the benefits to be derived instructionally through experiential learning activities and opportunities. From English and journalism (Deal and Beaver 1989) to foreign languages (Bryan 1991) and geography (Sublett 1989); from communications (Novak 1989; Schmidt et al. 1992; Thompsen 1991) to psychology (Megargee 1990), the literature suggests that faculty have adopted experiential learning activities to enhance traditional classroom learning to meet the needs of a changing society for their students.

Let's look at some of these. Zeuchner's formal culminating experience program requirement at California Polytechnic University at San Luis Obispo is directed at meeting these goals (1991). Every student in the speech-communications program participates in an experiential learning project such as officiating Lincoln-Douglas debates at local civic and service clubs. Experiential activity supports Shaver and Shaver's assumption that pedagogical theory in communications study that is passive and noninteractive is less successful and less satisfying than proactive and interactive learning (1995). They suggest that culture and communication "are one concept — inseparable from one another."

And Wattson views experiential learning as a process to ensure integration of such values (1992). Wattson continues, "The growth of communications internship programs designed to integrate communications theory with practical work experience is well documented" (p. 449). Each of these activities helps students master specific coursework and assists them to develop the personal development affective skills and competencies. Herdendorf uses individualized learning contracts to assist students to "learn critical international business concepts, skills, and other related learning" at Empire State College (1991, p. 3). Yes, according to Thorburn: "Most of the conventional assumptions about liberal learning and the nature of the liberal-arts college continue to have great value — . . . experiential learning does not contradict any of these assumptions . . . " (1990, p. 285).

Understanding Learning Theories and Cognitive Development

To more fully appreciate the value of experiential learning in the liberal-arts classroom, we as faculty need to take the time to understand the process of adult learning. Again, cognitively speaking, Kolb describes learning as proceeding through a cycle moving from: concrete experience to reflective observation; to abstract conceptualization; and finally to active experimentation. Effective experiential education must rely on an application of Kolb's Theory to meet Mosser's (1989) cognitive development outcomes, which include:

- To learn to consider various perspectives in problem solving;
- To learn alternative perspectives to decisionmaking processes;
- To reduce apprehension for dealing with complexity;
- To develop and use higher-order thinking skills in analyzing, synthesizing, and integrating information;
- To integrate prior knowledge from the classroom with new information gained in the real world;
- To think and operate at higher levels of complexity.

Faculty who do employ experiential learning activities do so, the literature suggests, for sound pedagogical reasons. Again, in describing as his main ingredient — "critical thinking" — for active learning, Greenberg emphasizes this new role for the active teacher as one who is interested in student learning through emphasizing the ability to think and solve complex problems, by structuring complex academic tasks for students to master.

Mosser reminds us of our students' personal development and cognitive development outcomes when considering the benefits of experiential education — those which are supported by Cross' "second force" (which was previously presented but deserves repetition):

Research in cognitive psychology suggests that experiential education has built into it many pedagogical advantages that must be artificially created in academic education (p. 22).

What kinds of active learning promote such cognitive development outcomes and goals? Anthony et al. (1990) describes the approaches taken by the faculty at Collin County Community College in several liberal-arts disciplines, including psychology and history. These faculty believe that "teaching should stimulate 'active learning' in which the student takes responsibility in the learning process" (p. 2). The institution's guiding philosophy, according to Anthony

To more fully appreciate the value of experiential learning in the liberal-arts classroom, we as faculty need to take the time to understand the process of adult learning.

et al., is drawn from Meyer's belief that "college instructors must strive to create a classroom atmosphere in which students' natural inquisitiveness can once again come to the fore" (1987, p. 9). Learner response and active participation is integral to curriculum planning at the college, which has integrated active experiential learning in the classroom and laboratory, including internships outside of the college, where appropriate.

Anthony et al. describe "six common features" inherent in the college's programs. They discuss:

> *Six common features, however, characterize the experiential components. First, they are learner-centered and student-directed; second, they place emphasis on problem solving, discovery, and inquiry; third, they emphasize practical applications of course content; fourth, they focus on holistic understanding; fifth, they are perception-based; and sixth, the emphasis is on the heuristic process — learning about learning* (1990, p. 4).

In Collin County Community College's psychology program, one will find a laboratory component coupled with ample journal writing and research applications, together with business-industrial internships. The laboratory component, a minimum of one hour per week, helps the student to integrate theoretical and practical elements of the courses. Internships, for college credit, help students relate their study to practical and business applications. Students work 20 hours per week, attend 16 hours of on-campus discussion groups during the semester, and write reaction papers. Faculty report that the challenges to the operation of the program have been in physical space for laboratories, coordination of laboratory equipment, and grading time for the increased practical work. However, through experiential learning, students "are free to concentrate on higher level development that includes synthesis, analysis, and the ability to integrate and apply knowledge" (Anthony et al. 1990, p. 6).

Antioch College in Ohio also takes a contextual learning approach to teaching psychology, according to Linn (1993). Herein, psychology students are required to participate in at least one work/study experience. These placements have included hospitals, a school for boys, and a fire department.

These placements must be closely supervised and coordinated with classroom work. However, Clements (1995) cites Haberman and Post, who indicate that: " . . . even when using field experiences, college students perceive their experiences selectively, ignoring information that is inconsistent with their previously held ideas" (1992, p. 16).

Alternatively, Megargee describes psychology internships whereby students extend out into the community to provide assistance to people and to gain firsthand experience about their chosen profession (1990). Yes, even in fields such as geography, instructional efforts can benefit from experiential learning (Sublett 1989). As Muldoon and Myrick have found in their Model U.N. program: "Students enjoy the experience because it challenges them intellectually, involves them in stimulating group activities, and exposes them to other ways of thinking — it's also a lot of fun" (1995, p. 98). Muldoon and Myrick credit Slavin (1989), who claims that less-structured cooperative techniques may be more effective than traditional individualistic techniques for high-level cognitive learning outcomes, such as identifying concepts, analysis of problems, judgment, and evaluation.

In yet another discipline at Collin County Community College, the history program has included experientially based work in the forms of video project requirements, giving the students an opportunity to become more creative and to apply critical thinking. Students plan their video, and then after discussing the idea with the faculty, actually execute the video production. Another project used has been analyses of popular television shows. For example, illustrating how history can come alive through such an analysis, the students imagine themselves as students in 2090 watching a 1953 *I Love Lucy* show and see an episode in which Ricky spanks Lucy. They then are asked to reflect on their experience to consider what their conclusion would be in 2090 on the status of women in the 1950s. And a third form of experiential learning for the students is historical recreation. Such projects have included the "Salem Witch Trials" and a "Lunch Counter Sit In." Other programs at Collin County Community College in which experiential learning is used includes sociology, mathematics, and accounting.

Likewise, in the writing area, Deal and Beaver describe intriguing experiential learning activities (1989). Deal and Beaver report study findings that indicate that professional writing internships produce more confident, motivated, marketable, and job-ready graduates.

Nontraditional Learners With Multitudes of Learning Styles and Needs

Stone and Wonser remind us that students learn "when they regard what they need to know as relevant to their lives" (1990, p. 3). Many experiential educators sense strongly that academic theory needs to be "tested" against experience by the student in order for learning to be both useful and meaningful (Moore 1990[a]). As described previously, our student body is changing. And as discussed earlier, many forces external to higher education are causing a revolution of sorts in the way in which we structure formal programs of learning in academia. Among them is an increasing ethnic, social, and economic diversity of our student bodies which, according to Johnson, necessitates a broader understanding of the purposes of education and the best ways to teach (1994). This changing student body demands relevancy in learning. It no longer is reasonable or acceptable to ask a student to trust that learning will "some day" be meaningful. The changing student body must see the relevancy before learning can occur.

Clarifying values, developing interpersonal skills, and developing empathy, tolerance, and respect for others are broad goals for all liberal-arts students. As offered by Cross, arguments for experiential learning include meeting the " . . . pressures of society" for well-educated workers and citizens capable of applying their knowledge to real-world problems (1994[b]). To accomplish this:

> *Students develop broader perspectives through comparisons; they learn to appreciate differences and similarities (sic: of other people) and increase their cultural awareness* (p. 7).

As we now are in a global community, to compete in the international marketplace our students will require language skills, cultural awareness, and international experience (Weinmann 1992). How can experiential learning-active learning make this possible in a liberal-arts course? Herein, Greenberg's construct of "climate" comes into focus. He offers that respect for diversity makes for a climate which is conducive to active involvement and which supports student motivation to learn. He suggests: " . . . the theoretical and data-based commentaries . . . have argued persuasively that students do better, learn more, and care more — get more actively involved if they feel valued as individuals" (p. 4). He pleads for "cooperation" (another of his ingredients for active learning) — for active teachers who help students to know each other, become familiar and comfortable with each other, and learn to use each other as resources (p. 5). This happens through "specific curriculum strategies," structures, activities, and assessment tools which help students learn in groups from each other as well as from the teacher (p. 5).

The literature suggests that such opportunities specifically aimed at minority and disadvantaged college students do exist. The New York State Senate Minority Summer Intern Program provides opportunities for students to learn by exploring firsthand the workings of state government alongside elected officials and their staffs. Another example is the Congressional Fellowship on Women and Public Policy, which provides an opportunity for women to study public-policy formulation. The "Learn and Serve America: Higher Education Program," sponsored by the Corporation for National and Community Service, makes available funds to support projects which make service an integral part of the educational process. Funding is granted based upon the project's objectives, which should include indicators of community impact, participant impact, and institutional impact.

Johnson also discusses the increasing average age of the college student and the increasing proportion of part-time college attendees. Effective teaching for these students comes from an understanding of these learners and their specific needs and learning conditions, which necessitates a rethinking of the best instructional strategies to accommodate their needs. And Oludaja discusses an experiential approach to teaching of intercultural communication for students who do not have opportunities to study regularly with students from different cultures (1993). The impetus for this, says Oludaja, quoting Kiser (1991), is that "most basic courses are more theoretically oriented, and devote less time to developing skills through actual intercultural interaction" (p. 3). Oludaja describes approaches such as "conversational partners" in which students from the communication course meet and converse with students from other cultures in an intensive training language course for Japanese exchange students. The program also uses international students as guest speakers and/or evening meetings with students from other more diverse campuses to celebrate diversity.

Added to the changes in student demographics is an ever-increasing application of new technology to life and work. Thus our world now is a much smaller one. We must live and work with different people and communicate effectively with them. Oftentimes the best way for this to happen is to leave the campus for formal study (Hayden 1992). Experiential learning in the forms of cooperative education, internships, externships, and other formal community-based learning experiences works to develop a sense of self in a society, and in a historical context, and with a cultural sophistication.

Changing Workplace Requirements
Throughout this report the issue of human coexistence has surfaced as a major goal of experiential education. To address this issue, educators have embraced the technique of service learning. Herein Greenberg discusses the issue of "curriculum" — another of his essential ingredients for active teaching. Specifically, he offers: " . . . the emphasis on critical thinking — one of the reasons for a focus on active learning — suggests rethinking curriculum" (p. 26).

Here Greenberg argues that the active teacher has to consider selecting content and defining curriculum organization in terms of the requirements suggested by a changing institutional context — a change from teacher as center to student as center. Why? There needs to be a shift toward concern for maintaining positive classroom climate, a shift toward more teamwork and cooperation in learning formats as well as peer relationships, and an emphasis on critical thinking and information transference (p. 26).

Raupp and Cohen offer commentary on the match of experiential learning and psychology (1992). They discuss volunteerism and internships. Specifically, "The psychology curriculum should encourage community service placements because they are consistent with psychology's values, good for students, and beneficial to the community" (p. 25).

The literature reveals that even at liberal-arts colleges that do not have formal experiential learning programs or opportunities, students often find ways to participate in experiential learning on their own. Thorburn reports that:

> College students instinctively recognize the value of
> experiential education, but it is not so readily appreciated by faculty members who are accustomed to the
> more traditional modes of instruction in the liberal-arts
> college (p. 284).

Many faculty encourage students to venture out into the community to provide some needed service and to experience the work as it really is. What kinds of programs exist and capitalize upon service learning? Raupp and Cohen's program at California State University at Bakersfield include volunteers as tutors in an elementary school and child-psychology volunteers at the "Human Corps" — a new initiative in California patterned after the National Service Corps. Section Four describes service learning in detail.

An Economic Necessity to More Closely Interface With Business and Community

A societal need exists for a well-educated workforce capable of competing in a global economy (Cross 1994[a]). Close working relationships or partnerships of academe with business and community is a relatively new concept. Certainly an overt gesture on the part of faculty to "build bridges" can be seen as unique — and to some extent this is happening across the nation — for several reasons. A prime reason is financial need. With decreasing public-education budgets and increasing costs to operate the academy, a need evolves to "lobby" the business and government sectors for support. Second, faculty always desire the benefits of grants and the institution seeks endowments. And, of course, we have an institutional mission to provide technology transfer to our constituencies. With this marketing effort comes the need to demonstrate "one's worth" in terms of value added to society. Experiential education partnerships have gone a long way toward attracting the kind of attention the institution of higher education wishes to enjoy.

What sorts of problems keep the academic and business communities apart? Certainly, prominent among the problems are perceived conflicts in the missions of both institutions. While there certainly are conflicting missions, there are areas wherein a quid pro quo exists for mutual collaboration. For the educational institution, faculty are able to provide learning activities out in the community which help students connect content to personal goals and needs.

Foreign-language educators are creatively using experiential learning in their programs not only to help students clarify their career objectives and make appropriate choices, but also to bridge academe and community. At Albion College, for instance, students are participating in experiential learning in the foreign languages through semester-long activities in foreign countries (see Thorburn 1990). Albion foreign-language students study abroad which, as stated by Thorburn, is: "Experiential learning in the truest sense but exceedingly compatible with time-honored standards for language instruction" (p. 256). Hence, he says that these programs take the students away from campus for one full semester, earn college credit, but they come back revitalized with a fuller appreciation for the world in which they live. Bryan describes the development and implementation of an internship requirement wherein students research and develop a project or perfect specific language skills within a framework or context of a specific field (1991). Therein, another objective of the internship is career counseling and career options clarification.

Ellis (1992) references Marra (1990) in describing a student-run advertising/public-relations agency at Oregon State University. Ellis relates:

> *Student competition, student ad clubs, and courses such as advertising campaigns provide students with simulated real-world experiences. But those experiences lack totality and remain incomplete. Further, they may represent a warp of what the real world means for a large percentage of students about to graduate and encounter the frustrating experience of finding a job in the field. To counter these problems, a student-run agency provides students with a total learning experience on a small advertising agency scale more in line with what they are likely to experience in their first jobs* (p. 1).

These junior/senior-level internships were in advertising

agencies and nonprofit organizations, for the most part. In the report Marra is quoted as stating:

Still, the actions of advertising educators reflect their support for merging student learning and experience with the real world practice of advertising (1990, p. 2).

If, in fact, advertising education should strive for this kind of relevance without forsaking its obligation to journalism and the larger breadth of a liberal-arts education, then a step in the right direction includes a student-run advertising agency course (p. 3).

Such experiences meet the learning outcomes discussed by Mosser, whereby use of more student-active methods of learning are largely self-directed and help students learn how to learn on the job and continue to learn over their lifetimes. Such experiences also help students to apply domain knowledge from coursework to real-world situations. It also exposes them to new technologies often not available on campus and helps them to develop interests in new fields of learning and to develop the vocabulary of the field.

In the communications arts, student-operated radio stations are a common form of experiential learning wherein students can develop such affective competencies together with technical skills. Thompsen describes one effort aimed at creating realistic student-run radio stations (1991). Within the communications disciplines, faculty are working to make these experiential learning activities as realistic as possible (Novak 1992; Cheslik 1989).

We even see students providing a campus community service through the operation of a real radio station (Rolls 1992). Novak describes a cooperative-education internship venture between the National Archives at West Georgia College (1989). Herein, students are able to approach the communications arts and broadcasting from a multidisciplinary humanistic perspective. Students use archived historical documents as the basis for broadcast program development.

We spoke earlier about the changing workplace, the changing economy, and the net effect of these changes on the college graduate. Yet, some would argue that a liberal-arts education is not a vocational education and hence, concerns of the workplace have no place in the liberal-arts classroom. This literature bears evidence about the benefits to the broad liberal-arts curriculum of experiential learning, however, and for the most part, experiential learning activities such as cooperative education tend all too often to be targeted to career and vocational programs.

Heermann (1973) cited the studies of Chase (1971), which established that the primary objective of experiential education through cooperative education was "career development" and that liberal-arts educators tended to view such "personal development" benefits as secondary to their educational missions. I argue to the contrary. A sound liberal-arts program is one that is successful in meeting a student's career goals. Career goals can, and often do, include academe. Mosser (1989) confirms these ideas and offers outcome indicators which include:

- To explore a career field
- To test career choices
- To confirm a choice of an academic major
- To gain a related work experience to give the student an edge in the job market
- To build a network of people who can assist in getting into graduate school or employment
- To earn money for an education
- To develop realistic understanding of the workplace
- To learn about the political nature of the workplace

It certainly is true, as indicated earlier, that "context and methods" within an academic discipline — and not pedagogical concerns — are foremost in the minds of most academicians. After all, that is what counts at promotion time.

Still, given an opportunity to make learning more successful for one's students, most faculty would consider improved pedagogical practices. Many liberal-arts faculty believe that a minimum amount of practical experience (for formal credit) and minimum standard of successful performance within a liberal-arts degree program are necessary to meet the goals of a program in the liberal arts as described by Mosser.

Faculty such as Deal and Beaver believe that courses that stop in the classroom and are only theoretical in nature may not help students believe in the efficacy of their formal educations when they compete in the job market upon graduation (1989). By example, the growth of "professional writing" programs and courses in English departments represents some attempt to offer new, vocationally oriented perspectives within traditional curricular frameworks (p. 1).

The Quid pro quo: Linking with and serving the community

The other side of the quid pro quo is the benefit in kind to the business community for such cooperation. Among the benefits derived is a chance to help develop tomorrow's citizens and workers and recruit the best of them to the business organization and, of course, the civic pride amassed to the organization from such participation.

Concerns About Selection, Control and Evaluation of the Learning Process

What makes the use of experiential learning activities often so difficult for the college educator to implement? First and perhaps foremost, according to Moore:

> *Experiential education potentially constitutes a fundamental challenge to the traditional definitions of knowledge and the historical arrangements of power on which the university operates* (p. 279).

From a college president's perspective, Mosser discusses several salient reasons why experiential learning, including cooperative education, is a necessity across the liberal-arts curriculum (1990). Among these is the changing demographics of the college learner — and specifically, the growing numbers of older adult students. Mosser cites the fact that between 1969 and 1984, the adult population attending undergraduate education grew 33 percent.

Experiential education facilitates a diversity of educational experiences and programming to meet the changing learning styles of these changing learners. It also can provide a "fast track" for educational achievement for some of these learners. Or it can be a means by which to "learn and earn" for others. Herein, another one of Greenberg's active-learning ingredients — "center" — comes into play. The active teacher must step back and look at the primary goals and purposes of the institution. Students must be at the center of the learning process; learning is the most important result.

Experiential education facilitates a diversity of educational experiences and programming to meet the changing learning styles of these changing learners.

Teachers must devise structures and activities to place students at the center and to define quality by what they do, not by what the teacher does. Thorburn (1990) offers additional suggestions for the college's provost or chief academic officer. The college's chief academic officer "must first recognize that field experience is a part of the curriculum, carries credit, requires faculty advisement and supervision (thus classroom release time), and involves units that might otherwise be taken in a conventional classroom situation" (p. 285).

Additionally, Goldstein cites specific legal issues that must be recognized by the university and dealt with accordingly (1990). These include:

- Contracts of enrollment. He states that in experiential education, students may assume learning outcomes very different from those envisioned by the college. Hence, learning contracts can become very useful devices to mitigate against potential challenges and litigation.
- Liability of acts of the student. The college cannot afford to be held liable for acts of the student within the greater community when engaged in cooperative education. Therefore careful supervision and insurance might be considered.
- Equal opportunity and civil rights. All students must be given equal chances for experiential learning and activities such as cooperative education. This issue surfaces when making decisions about who qualifies for cooperative education.

Raupp and Cohen discuss the time-intensive nature of supervising psychology interns within a community. They discuss the need to validate work sites, interview intern preceptors, ensure written agreements are adhered to, debrief student interns and preceptors concerning progress, rectify problems, and grade students at program completion. Additional suggestions offered include exercising caution where controversial placements are concerned — specifically preceptors who, in the opinion of the instructor, might not meet college standards, or safety concerns and issues including the work environment, and, of course, confidentiality of student records and student intern understanding of the need to keep business matters confidential. Finally good relationships between student interns, their preceptors, clients, and college faculty need to be maintained.

Thorburn highlights certain additional roles that must be accounted for in making experiential learning, including cooperative education, successful and workable. These include assignment of specific responsibilities for: (1) a project director who will serve as an administrative point of contact within and external to the college with business and industry and the community for issue resolution and public relations, as well as with placement of interns; and (2) faculty supervisory assignments for cooperative education. Oftentimes a sharing of the load between faculty is most workable. Appropriate teaching-load adjustments must be made to ensure that the on-the-job portions of the experiential learning and cooperative-education activity is working smoothly. Thorburn states:

> *Load reduction is almost as good for morale as money is. If such a load adjustment for an experiential learning program seems unjustified, just compare the number of students involved and the objectives they attain through it with other courses regularly offered that may enroll no more than six to ten students* (p. 288).

Thorburn offers further suggestions concerning the role of faculty: "Faculty members must . . . make the basic policy decisions about what kind of field experience, where, and for how long . . . " (p. 285). Hence, the use of experiential learning on a wide-scale basis all-too-often is met with resistance on the part of departmental or college faculty committees and scorned upon in evaluating teaching for tenure or promotion purposes.

In closing . . .

Through this review of the literature, the various kinds of experiential learning experiences present in most all academic programs have been highlighted. Certainly experiential education has demonstrated benefits for enhancing liberal-arts studies. As Moore relates:

> *Field-based education, in which students are thought to learn through experience in 'real-world' settings, tends to vacillate in its conception of knowledge. The classic*

*definition of experiential education refers to 'learning
activities that engage the learner directly in the phenomena being studied'* (Sage 1981, p. 275).

As competition for students increases within the higher education arena and students more carefully scrutinize colleges
and programs across all disciplines for indicators of success
of graduates in their chosen professions, faculty are more
seriously considering the values of experiential learning as
an integral part of their programs. Why cause students to
suffer through learning? As Smythe cautions: "Only in the
liberal arts has experiential learning yet to establish itself as
a fully respectable, universal element of the curriculum"
(1990, p. 294).

And . . .

*Not that moral education should proceed entirely
through the 'school of hard knocks,' as it is appropriate-
ly called. Theoretical study and critical thought are
essential as sources of form, structure, and discipline.
But in the absence of real acts with real consequences,
the discipline is incomplete, and the moral aspect of
liberal education becomes as abstract and as remote
from the practical as is metaphysics. This is where experiential education makes its most profound contribution to the liberal arts — and this is where the liberal
arts most need a healthy dose of real experience*
(Smythe 1990, p. 306).

Thus, as Moore sums up:

*. . . experiential learning offers as good an opportunity
as we have in higher education to create a critical pedagogy, a form of discourse in which teachers and students
conduct an unfettered investigation of social institutions, power relations and value commitments* (p. 280).

Therefore, according to Thorburn:

*Experiential learning is incompatible with more tradi-
tional learning only if the academy is incompatible
with the society of which it is a part* (p. 292).

THE PROGRAMS: PROFESSIONAL AND
TECHNICAL DISCIPLINES

Student learning through planned experientially based activities is a most relevant issue to educators in the professional and technical disciplines. The literature is replete with discussions of experiential learning applications and program analyses spanning the areas of law; teacher education; medicine; health care and social work; and science, engineering and technology — and at associate, baccalaureate, and master's levels (Baxter Magolda 1993; Cantor 1993; Gardner and Kozlowski 1993; Hightower 1993; Roebuck and Hochman 1993; Russell 1993; Schmitigal 1993; Dore, Epstein, and Herrerias 1992; Rosenbaum et al. 1992; Washington 1992; Acosta 1991; Anthony 1991; Meade 1991; Paulter 1991; Cayan and Jacquart 1990; Gettys 1990; Joslin and Ellis 1990; MacIsaac 1990; Paulter 1990).

And while experiential education is not new or unique as an instructional methodology in those disciplines involving practical skills training (cooperative education in associate-degree programs, for example), it deserves an analytical review in the professional fields such as teacher education and health sciences which have come under scrutiny in recent years. Let's begin in the law and education professions.

Linking Theory to Practice: Cross-Disciplinary Pedagogical and Instructional Issues

The study of lawyering has its genesis in experiential learning. Historically, law students have "read for the bar," clerking for lawyers to learn how to be a lawyer. Probably the best known of these "clerks" is Abraham Lincoln. Much like apprenticeship, the value of this form of contextual learning in the art of lawyering is best expressed in the comments of Givelber et al.:

> The impact of contextualist insights on legal pedagogy is threefold. First, and most important, context is pre-eminent over all else in structuring experience and its cognitive counterpart, learning. Accordingly, to learn lawyering competencies . . . a law student must experience or be in the complex, situational context of a lawyer (1995, p. 10).

While higher education practices over the many decades has moved toward more "traditional" lecture and recitation forms of teaching, some institutions, such as Northeastern University, have maintained a requirement for externships and other contextual experiences as part of their formal educational programs. This active engagement in learning is favored well by NU law students and professors. In fact, law professors also immerse themselves in lifelong contextual learning to keep abreast of the art of lawyering through law-office sabbaticals (1995).

Experiential learning in teacher education: Preparing teachers for service in a new world order

We now focus our discussion on programs in teacher education. Probably no other single professional preparation program reflects the magnitude and breadth of concerns exposed in the previous sections concerning preparation of students to meet the challenges of a new world order. For it is the teachers of tomorrow who will bear the responsibility for preparing intellectually equipped critical thinkers for the next century. Hence, the teacher education programs must be examined and retooled, if necessary, to provide those needed intellectual challenges to its cadre of prospective teachers to mold them into lifelong learners with the requisite skills and knowledge, ready for the challenge.

Yes, the academic community is taking a closer look at public education and the myriad of problems confronting the public schools. As a result, more attention is being paid to the methods by which we prepare our teachers for service in the schools. Numerous reports on the condition of schools and professional teacher preparation have been released (see the *Holmes Report* and the National Board for Professional Teaching Standards).

In this regard, Taylor and Samaras (1994), Russell (1993), and Meade (1991), among others, specifically note the weaknesses in the traditional approaches to clinical training of preservice teachers (an essential component of the preparation of teachers) and offer alternatives toward its solution. A focus on proactive and interactive learning for preservice teachers is needed so they may become proactive and interactive.

It appears that specific types of experiential learning activities are favored in certain programs and disciplines. The forms that experiential education takes in the professions warrant discussion and analysis. In the education professions, field experiences such as internships and practicums are prevalent. Taylor and Samaras stress that these field experiences must be redesigned and administered to ensure teacher candidates can glean the full meaning of teaching and learning (1994). To do so, they have introduced into their program a junior-year internship to bring practice closer to the theoretical goals of the teacher education program at Catholic University. Their program is based upon four criteria they deem necessary for effective "reflective teacher education" programs. They describe their curriculum as based upon the earlier thoughts of Valli and Taylor:

1. Incorporates reflection throughout the program;
2. incorporates an epistemology which is rigorous, critical and experience based;
3. involves problems or issues which are normatively situated; and
4. employs instructional strategies which progressively link knowledge with action (1987, p. 3).

To be successful, "reflective" teacher education programs must ensure that the total learning environment for both the teacher interns and the participating school's students is realistic and mutually beneficial. Therefore, Meade calls for "lead schools" as initially prescribed by the Carnegie Task Force on Teaching as a Profession. These schools would be specifically, he states:

> . . . devoted to teacher training and development as well as to student instruction. . . . The college faculty members should serve as professional peers to selected classroom teachers who would function as clinical supervisors (pp. 667-68).

Examination of "reflection-in-action" theories has been an area of ongoing research as indicated by Gettys (1990). The University of Tennessee at Knoxville conducted a case study of five-year teacher education programs in which the fifth year was devoted to full-time internship work. Gettys, as well as Boyer (1990), reported favorable results from this two-phase approach to professional teacher preparation.

The program (which is gaining in popularity) is a two-phase process. The undergraduate years of study focus on a liberal-arts education and a strong subject-matter preparation. The fifth year, thus, is the professional year. The philosophical underpinning for this five-year program is credited to the Holmes plan (1986), which called for strengthening both academic and pedagogical preparation. Gettys outlines the University of Tennessee at Knoxville's perspective as follows:

> *We wanted to prepare talented people with degrees in liberal arts for secondary school teaching through an intensive internship. Interns would spend ten weeks in the summer taking methods courses, learning the theory behind successful classroom teaching. Then they would spend a year in the classroom, teaching three classes a day and performing other teacher responsibilities, such as lunchroom supervision. A selected teacher at the intern's assigned school would be on hand to advise and help the intern. We hoped to show that a successful alternative certification program combines intensive coursework, classroom training, and guidance from experienced teachers and education faculty. We also hoped to demonstrate that a full year of teaching before certification was a good idea for all education students* (Wisniewski 1990, p. 4 in Gettys 1990).

The Catholic University program also was similarly restructured to have teacher candidates spend a concentrated amount of time in the field classroom. The junior year is reconceptualized as two professional semesters. The field experience occurs during the first professional semester. The second professional semester consists of the major methods courses and a half-day practicum to provide the concentrated period of time in classrooms with children and their teachers. These efforts are aimed at meeting two complementary objectives on the part of Catholic University's faculty:

> *. . . a framework for better preparing those entering their student teaching experience to both understand how to plan instruction and reflect upon their efforts and university involvement in professional renewal with teachers who work with our students* (Taylor, Samaras, and Gay 1994, p. 6).

Regarding the appropriate length for a professional internship, Meade also calls for a full-time, yearlong paid experience for preservice teachers, not unlike a medical-school internship. He offers:

> In my judgment, an entire school year would be optimal, so that the interns could come to understand the full context — the ebb and flow of schooling over the months.

> Moreover, those undertaking a teaching internship should be paid for it, as are interns in such fields as medicine, architecture, law, and business. As interns, preservice teachers are both learning and working. That work should be acknowledged with compensation (p. 667).

Mastering learning theories and cognitive development

How teachers master the principles of human learning is an imperative issue to consider. Professional teacher preparation requires ample opportunities for "reflection-in-action" for aspiring teacher candidates, so claims Russell (1993) and Catelli (1995). Based upon the prior work of Schon (1983) and Kennedy (1987), Russell draws constructive parallels to the field of teacher education. She argues that professional expertise comes about through learning from experience. And she elaborates:

> Casting expertise in the domain of deliberate action generates goals that are different from those in programs based on technical skills or theory and general principles. Foremost among these goals are greater thoughtful control of action by the professional and greater stimulation of thought by action (pp. 60-61).

Catelli adds that it is the rigorous questioning followed by constructive dialogue that causes students in an action-oriented learning situation to compare their current experiences to their previous knowledge and experience base to challenge their values and add to their practical wisdom and experience. Baxter Magolda adds from her findings of a study of how graduate students develop contextual knowledge:

> *Findings indicated five major themes: (1) students value opportunities to think and explore for themselves, to struggle with ideas, and to formulate and support their own opinions; (2) students are interested in connecting their beliefs with their own lives and identities; (3) learning environments in which students' knowledge and experiences are central facilitate the making of such connections by students; (4) such learning environments are characterized by teachers and students taking on roles as equal partners who mutually respect each other; and (5) peers are also viewed as equal partners whose sharing and exchange of perspectives enhances exploration of what to believe* (1993, p. 1).

Cognitive development through experiential learning is described as happening through a continuum, as previously offered by Kolb. A theory of ecological learning, predicated upon the constructs of Bruner, Dewey, Edelman, Schoen, and others is offered by Baker (1994). Argued from the professional vantage point of the preparation of practitioners for the legal profession but certainly not limited to such professional preparation, Baker suggests: "According to the precepts of a contextualist pedagogy, to 'learn' a practice domain one must situate oneself in the domain engaging its authentic dilemmas and activity integrating its multiple sources of information" (p. 291). She describes a contextualist's view of situated, functionally engaged cognition as having five principal features:

1. Cognition is historically and enactively situated in a physical body and a social/cultural context.
2. Cognition is simultaneous, holistic, and predominantly subconscious as well as conscious.
3. Cognition focuses on the flow of "events" in a fluid field of stability and change.
4. Cognition prefers active social practice which ordinarily evidences both functionality and authenticity.
5. Cognition is "pluralistic," attending to multiple sources and choosing among many plausible interpretations and actions.

Paulter (1991) builds upon a framework for clinical experience development which is based on specific goals to be mastered in the continuum and which he enumerates as: (1) assessing career development; (2) refining school goals; (3) practicing in realistic settings; (4) developing competence; and (5) promoting personal professional development. These five purposes are extrapolated from Daresh's (1987) and Boser's (1990) rationale for a practicum.

To ensure capitalizing upon sound cognitive development principles, Paulter developed his framework into a three-level program plan (based upon Milstein's [1990] proposed clinical experience sequencing) commencing with an aid-ship and segueing into an internship and finally into an associateship. He suggests certain operational guidelines for internship programs, including job content analysis; alignments of the theory/practice relationship; and selection of appropriate learning experiences.

As justification for his multilevel approach to experiential learning, Paulter offers the following comments:

According to the precepts of a context-ualist peda-gogy, to 'learn' a practice do-main one must situate oneself in the domain engaging its authentic dil-emmas and activity inte-grating its multiple sources of information."

> *It would seem essential that such beginning experience serve at least two major purposes. First, that the experiences provided assist the student in assessing his/her own career commitment to this area of future endeavor. This should be considered of personal value to the student. Second, the experiences should assist the faculty in assessing the abilities of the students involved in the program. Is this the type of person that will make it as a school administrator? At the same time how can the experiences be planned so that they align with the theory part of the program (p. 12).*

Teachers gain exposure to diversity. Paull et al. (1995) describe the efforts undertaken at Pepperdine University together with the Los Angeles Unified School District to restructure a program in teacher education to better prepare administrators for service in an urban school district known for its richness in diversity. Included in the revised program are a yearlong field practicum and a reflective triweekly seminar.

Likewise, MacIsaac (1990) describes a teacher induction partnership program at the University of Northern Colorado.

He too touts this effort as a "reality-based educational experience" for preservice teachers. This program features a mentor/protege model similar to the University of Tennessee program. Teacher-interns also work full time in participating schools, attend seminars on campus, and earn 10 graduate credits toward a master's degree and a stipend. This program is designed to facilitate a smooth transition from beginning or reentry teachers to experienced professionals. MacIsaac states:

> *The program was designed to address alarming dropout rates of teachers nationally, provide a framework for beginning teachers to enter the profession successfully, and foster interaction between the University and Colorado school districts* (p. 6).

And MacIsaac further describes his situation:

> *The program provides an orientation for mentors, principals, and partner teachers; graduate seminars; a three person support team for each partner teacher; legal contracts between all parties stipulating roles and responsibilities; graduate courses for mentors; full-time university staff who conduct regular classroom observations and instruct seminars; release time for partner teachers to observe other teachers, attend conferences, etc.; — all aimed at creating a safe context for personal and professional growth, experimentation, and reflection* (p. 4).

Meade further offers:

> *Finally, the clinical school ought to be a place that fosters instructional diversity, a place in which one will find a variety of legitimate pedagogical or instructional practices rather than one form that dominates or is mandated* (p. 667).

Internships in teacher education need not be just for preservice teachers. Educational administrators can benefit as well. Paulter reports on the findings and conclusions of a joint study of the University Council for Educational Administration and the National Policy Board for Educational Administration (1990). These bodies report that there be: "one full year of academic residency and one full year of field residency in the Ed.D. preparation program" (p. 6). While a study of UCEA member schools indicated that most do have internship requirements, the length and approach vary considerably. And,

> *Few institutions seem to come near the goal of the National Policy Board for Educational Administration in requiring one full-year of field residency for all students* (1989, p. 15).

Joslin and Ellis describe a school administrator preparation program designed to diversify responsibility, integrate the theory-practice relationship, and develop leadership of its students (1990). They express concerns that educational administration students were likely to approach their first assignments full of theories and lacking in practical skills. The internship model described occurs over a yearlong period and includes a student-developed individualized plan. Reflective seminars, on campus, are framed around Gardner's (1990), Quinn's (1988), and Burns' (1978) leadership theories.

Paulter describes the educational administration program at SUNY Buffalo which consists of three levels. He describes this first "aidship" component as an observation of administrators in action. About midway into the program, the internship portion begins which, it is argued, should include a full-time experience. The third component is called an "associateship" and is usually a group-activity project (1991, p. 7). Paulter justifies this multilevel approach through Milstein, who offers:

> *The purposes of clinical experiences are to enable students to be exposed to reality-based programs that permit a balance between learning about and learning how and that are rooted in a solid foundation of learning why* (p. 9).

Meade (1991) adds:

> *The clinical phase of teacher education needs to be a shared responsibility among three equal partners: schools and school systems, colleges and universities,*

and professional organizations of teachers. These part-
ners need to develop clinical training for prospective
teachers (p. 669).

Experiential education often can serve as a catalyst to bring
together organizations which share common goals. Roebuck
and Hochman describe such a partnership of teacher education and community service agencies (1993). Butler
University's social-studies teacher education program joined
forces with Junior Achievement of Central Indiana to provide upper-class students of elementary education methods
with an opportunity to experiment with teaching the Junior
Achievement Business Basics curriculum. Herein these students gained pedagogical experience through integrating
social-studies methods with other curriculum elements and
also served the greater community (p. 76).

These authors report that their students gained classroom
management experience and a better understanding of the
adolescent and the need to modify instructional processes to
meet learner needs. Finally, MacIsaac concludes in highlight-
ing the overall success of his particular program for the
community at large:

> *To conclude, an induction program grounded in a*
> *university/school district context of collaboration is*
> *much more than a vehicle to address the needs of the*
> *beginning teacher. It is a catalyst for change fostered*
> *through relationships designed and facilitated by com-*
> *mitted individuals. The identity, philosophy, and design*
> *continues to be influenced by local needs and expecta-*
> *tions of emerging teachers as well as national concerns*
> *and awareness about induction. The UNC model cur-*
> *rently provides equal ownership and responsibility of*
> *the induction process to the university and public*
> *schools* (p. 11).

As a final argument for development of teacher education
programs that capitalize upon experiential learning
practicums, Russell sums with:

> *If reflection-in-action can be developed as a strategy for*
> *learning from experience, then beginning teachers may*
> *have more confidence in their reactions to experience*

and fewer frustrations when practice seems so unrelat-
ed to theory and principles. The development of exper-
tise in teaching is closely related to experience and
action (1993, p. 61).

Next we will look at the experiential learning issues in
health care and social work, science and engineering, and
technology professions.

The Health Care and Social Work Professions

Inasmuch as technical competence and a full comprehen-
sion of the environment in which the work takes place is
necessary to the beginning physician, health care practition-
er or social worker, the literature documents that experiential education through clinical experiences is an accepted
practice and in many cases required by the cognizant
accrediting agencies.

Much like the legal profession, physician training has a
long-standing tradition in experiential education. The med-
ical internship is a requisite and recognized part of basic
education for physicians. Within specialty care training,
Stross describes a primary care preceptorship in which primary care contextual learning is provided to physicians in
training through clerkships to help them fully understand
and manage the problems in primary care (1995).

Washington (1992); Dore, Epstein, and Herrerias (1992);
and Acosta (1991) speak to the benefits and issues of experiential learning in professional preparation programs.
Washington writes: "Results showed that there was a significant change in attitude of the subjects (sic: students) towards
their skills . . . resulting from their . . . experience" (p. 7).

Acosta's experiential education research efforts at Auburn
University demonstrated the utility of this instructional
process for undergraduate students in the health professions.
She offers:

The experiential learning model provides a framework
which helps health educators understand the various
ways through which individuals learn, develop and
acquire knowledge that is not only cognitively retained
but also behaviorally apparent. The role of the health
educator is to guide the individual in reaching a solu-

tion to a problem. Using the experiential learning and critical inquiry framework, the health educator does not solve the problem for the individual; instead, s/he acts as a facilitator in the exploration of alternative ways to solve the problem (p. 10).

Acosta adds:

The experiential learning and critical inquiry framework grounded in reflection is useful in the creation of individualized learning experiences. The goal of critical inquiry and experiential learning lies in the reflection of the learning processes through which the outcomes are accomplished (p. 6).

In the social work programs, internships are prominent forms for experiential learning and the activities are structured to professional standards. Dore et al. (1992) discuss the benefits of experiential learning via internships to the preparation of social workers. They offer that the credit-earning fieldwork components of social work programs long have been an essential component of professional training in schools of social work (p. 353). Objectives of fieldwork components of these programs include:

- Development of the ability to discern in humans and in concrete situations the facts and concepts with which students elsewhere have become intellectually familiar.
- Mastery of the essential elements of social work in practice.
- Modification of certain typical attitudes that interfere with efficiency in the practice of social work.
- Development of certain personality traits in the student whose adaptation in certain ways makes for more effective social case work (Lee and Kenworthy 1929, p. 191) as cited in Dore et al. 1992 (p. 354).

Dore et al. conceptualize the fieldwork component as providing their students with an opportunity to experience themselves in the social work role and thus confront personal obstacles to their professional development. They cite Reynolds, who stated that the fieldwork experience helps a student develop a "professional attitude" — hence, "the ability to make the client and his/her situation the center of attention automatically and without prejudice" (1942, p. 354). Dore et al. reiterate Skolnik's comments that "the field experience as the primary arena for integrating knowledge and values with skills — the professional person takes shape and is shaped" (1989, p. 355).

Science and Engineering

America faces a critical shortage of educated and trained people in the sciences and engineering. To ensure and promote student successes in these disciplines, Laws, Rosborough, and Poodry (1995) discuss the value of experiential learning in the teaching of introductory physics. They view the constructivist nature of the learning experience as positively affecting a student's critical-thinking processes. It is especially useful, they argue, for ensuring success and thus retention of nontraditional science students — women and minorities.

Hayman (1993) presents the business perspective of experiential learning in the sciences and engineering. She discusses Boeing's efforts at partnering with universities to produce a "world-class" workforce. She paraphrases a corporate executive at Boeing offering that if a void exists between academe and industry, this can create a situation where schools are preparing students who do not meet the needs of the employers. Colleges of engineering reportedly are working more closely with engineering firms to offer students internships in engineering fields.

Changing Students and Their Changing Needs

Students entering the professions are a microcosm of society itself. They represent, if not in direct proportion, certainly in significant numbers, those minority segments of society described earlier. Experiential learning in the teaching of professional disciplines assists these students in succeeding, oftentimes as first-generation professionals. Professional, technical, and graduate studies students tout the benefits of experiential education as part of their programs. Refer again to Baxter Magolda's (1993) assessment of student feelings toward experiential learning as a process for developing contextual learning. In a longitudinal study of 25 postbaccalaureate students, she found evidence of positive benefits of experiential education for graduate studies programs.

O'Brien looked at college students' employment activities

during their years of college study (1993). She found that 60 percent of all college students do seek out experiential learning through work while engaging in collegiate study. Certainly students from lower socioeconomic backgrounds need these work activities to survive. If the professional programs in which they are matriculated require these experiential learning field-based activities, this becomes an added benefit.

But of what academic benefit is such work? Anthony discusses the benefits of involvement in learning in terms of its impact on the professional and technical student's outcomes (1991). Gardner and Kozlowski describe the findings of a study conducted by the Collegiate Employment Research Institute of Michigan State University to determine if experiential education experiences better prepare students to assume functional roles more quickly upon initial employment (1993). They, in fact, found that students profited by acquiring more effective learning strategies, accruing greater knowledge, and adjusting to a new organizational life more quickly.

Schmitigal discusses her study of 22 students in business communications who engaged in a collaborative project with several Sault Saint Marie, Mich., businesses (1993). These student volunteers provided public service to these firms. The results indicated that the students did, in fact, believe that they had profited by learning the importance of business-communications skills in solving real-life business problems. Anthony offers: "The more time, energy, and effort they invest in the learning process and the more intensely they engage in their own education, the greater will be their growth and achievement, their persistence in college, and the more likely they will continue their learning after college" (1991, p. 391).

Business and Community Issues and Concerns
As it relates to preparation for the professions, all too many studies indicate that America indeed is in trouble in terms of workforce preparedness to meet 21st-century workplace demands. Portwood and Naish discuss a major and significant finding of their study as the concerns expressed by cooperative employers about global competitiveness of U.S. businesses and their workforce and the need for business-college linkages for professional workforce education and training through experiential education activities (1993). Experiential education offers a solution, at least in part, to that dilemma.

And Soter discusses the business community's concerns with worker training and educational-business community relationships (1993). Soter describes several experiential learning approaches in which business can engage with universities, including mentoring. Soter further offers, "The business community is taking a proactive approach to change the way its future workers are being educated. By joining with schools in educational partnerships, many businesses are finding that tremendous results can be accomplished through teamwork" (p. 11). Similarly, employers appeared also to benefit by creating a more qualified applicant pool from which to recruit and select new employees.

Technology Programs

And what about lower-division experiential learning for lower-division students? In an era in which it has been documented that workers need a minimum of two years of postsecondary education to compete in a global economy, the means by which we structure higher education to ensure that our technology students do succeed in meeting or exceeding two years of college-level education and training is a necessary goal. Program models to meet this goal do exist. One experiential learning model which is receiving renewed interest in the literature is apprenticeship (Rosenbaum et al. 1992). Another is business and industry partnerships with lower-division higher education (Hightower 1993).

Anthony describes the efforts of both faculty and administration at Collin County Community College in Texas to develop and institutionalize experiential learning into programs across the curriculum. Administrators at Collin County Community College express the following philosophy toward student involvement in the learning process:

> *Our goal was to be unique, not in what we taught, but in how we taught it. We set out to design an educational environment that would provide students with maximum opportunity to become actively involved in the learning process. One of the major decisions taken by the college to integrate active learning into the curriculum was to establish an experiential component in all disciplines, including liberal-arts courses. The focus is on the how rather than merely the what, and on inquiry, critical analysis, synthesis, and abstract logical thinking* (p. 393).

Anthony continues:

> *The specific structure of the experiential component
> purposefully remains fluid and individualized accord-
> ing to the needs of the subject area and creativity of the
> teaching faculty. "Hands on" laboratory experiences
> are provided in most courses. Beyond the classroom,
> internships and cooperative work experience programs
> provide additional student involvement* (p. 391).

And Portwood and Naish describe the college's efforts at
developing programs such as Middlesex County College in
New Jersey's collaborative agreement with Ford Motor Co. to
provide associate's degree automotive-technology students
with credit-bearing and paid internships in automotive dealerships as part of their degree study (1993). They discuss the
process as a negotiated joint effort in which the students are
selected by the college for admission and approved by the
company for cooperative training. Curriculum development
becomes a shared activity with business and industry, thus
ensuring up-to-date programs. The dealership then employs
the students full time after successful graduation of a program of study which incorporates classroom education with
structured on-the-job training.

Apprenticeship links business and education
In lower-division programs, Rosenbaum et al. discuss the
movement toward apprenticeship as a form of experiential
learning for structured workforce education and training
(1992). Cantor extends the argument for experiential learning
through apprenticeship as a method to deliver quality education and training and a catalyst for linking business and
industry and higher education to deliver high-technology
education and training (1993; 1992[b]). In fact, programs
including fire-science technology have practicum experiences
(e.g., apprenticeships) integrated within the degree program.
And six major features characterize these experiences. These,
according to the author, are: Activities are learner-centered
and student-directed; they place the emphasis on problem-
solving, discovery, and inquiry; they emphasize practical
applications of course content; they focus on holistic understanding; they are perception-based; and finally, the emphasis is on heuristic processes — learning about learning.

Cantor describes apprenticeship programs in which business and government have provided the opportunity for community college students to study on the job under the direct supervision of master technicians, as preceptors, as part of a college degree program (1994; 1992[b]). Cantor describes other like collaborative agreements between community colleges and automotive manufacturers, including General Motors, Chrysler, Toyota, Honda, and their participating dealerships (1993; 1991). In each of these cases, the manufacturer has a model curriculum guide to share with the college to ensure training to industry standards and requirements. Training also is available for college faculty in the manufacturer's products. Additionally, equipment, facility updating, and other assistance is provided to the college as an incentive to cooperate with the firm. In many cases, scholarship funding is available for minority students selected to participate in the cooperative education arrangement.

Cantor also describes like programs in the shipbuilding industry, fire service, and electrical and mechanical trades. Apprenticeship as a form of experiential education is alive and well in other professions as well, including nursing and allied health sciences, office technologies, and law enforcement and government services.

Educational foundations

Formation of alliances for higher education experiential learning with business and industry is an interesting and necessary part of a review of this topic. Partnerships between community colleges and local business and industry in which experiential education serves as a catalytic function, providing both real-life education and training to students as well as fostering community economic development, can be found in the literature. One prime example can be witnessed in the Professional Automotive Training Center at Shoreline Community College in Seattle (Hightower 1993).

This joint venture involves some 230 local automotive dealers, the automotive trade association representing the area new-car dealers, automotive manufacturers, and the state of Washington. The partnership is incorporated as a nonprofit educational foundation under IRS Title 501[c]3.

Students work in the dealership during alternate quarters and attend classes in the other quarters. The program boasts a 100 percent placement rate for associate of arts degree

In lower-division programs, Rosenbaum et al. discuss the movement toward apprenticeship as a form of experiential learning as a method to deliver quality education and training and a catalyst for linking business and industry and higher education to deliver high-technology education and training.

recipients in automotive service technology. The PSADA-
Shoreline Community College partnership, according to
Hightower, " . . . shows that it is possible to . . . provide
solid basic skills and specialized technical skills that respond
to technological innovation and social change" (p. 13).

Tech prep and other career education movements
Another catalyst for educational alliances, termed "Tech
Prep," is an articulated partnership between secondary and
postsecondary educational institutions and business and industry. It is an articulation process involving coordination of
curricula across two or more institutions to ensure graduates
possess the prerequisite knowledge and skills required for
employment in a chosen occupation or profession. Lankard
(1991) cites Robertson-Smith (1990), who describes Tech Prep
as an "advanced skills" articulation model "because it enables
students to use the time saved through coordinated course
work to acquire the more advanced occupational knowledge
and skill required by changing technologies" (p. 1).

The time saved also can be used for on-the-job training in
cooperative placements, as is happening in such a program
operated between Lehman College, Bronx Community
College, and the New York City Schools, in a Tech Prep
arrangement for health-careers programs with participating
Bronx County health care agencies. And Lankard cites
Watkins' (1989) discussion of the streamlining of the transfer
process — from secondary to postsecondary career education — or from associate's degree to bachelor's degree study
— because of the elimination of unnecessary duplication of
program content, which ensures continuity in education and
training and increased achievement of minority students
which this kind of "2+2+2" arrangement promotes.

Portwood and Naish discuss partnerships as a most necessary agreement for successful work-study arrangements
(1993). Tech Prep articulation processes truly are aimed at
establishing and promoting partnerships at all levels — from
associate's degree through graduate study.

Several California State University colleges of education
and participating public school districts including CSU
Fresno and the State Center Community College District
have used articulated 2+2+2 arrangements to recruit minority
teacher candidates into teacher education programs.
Students begin study at the high school. These students then

gain admission to an associate's degree program at a neighboring community college and progress onto a CSU program in teacher education. Throughout the several years of study these students participate in a truly reflective work-study experience at various levels in a participating school system.

Administrative Issues and Concerns

What problems and thoughts do college administrators have about experiential learning in the professional, technical, science and engineering, and graduate studies disciplines? Certainly, as was discussed in Section 2, issues of faculty release time, student liability, program development costs, and supervision of students at the job site are paramount in the minds of administration and faculty. The literature suggests that faculty in the professional and technical disciplines do not hold the beliefs of their academic subjects' counterparts about the inappropriateness of experiential learning in their classrooms. Much to the contrary. These faculty support experiential learning. Their concerns tend to be more in the areas of effective supervision and control of the learning processes through classroom and field experiences.

For example, Taylor, Samaras, and Gay discuss three pitfalls in the field experience that should be addressed by teacher educators supervising a field experience component in teacher education programs (1994). These are:

1. Familiarity, or the tendency to unquestionably trust that which is familiar from personal experience.
2. The two-worlds pitfall, or the fact that goals and expectations of the university and the classroom often are different and at odds with each other.
3. The pitfall of cross purposes, the fact that classrooms are set up for teaching children rather than teachers and what is reinforced is adaption to the here and now.

These pitfalls tend to limit what is learned from experience (p. 2).

In closing . . .

Discussion of these issues of planning, supervision, faculty compensation, student recruitment, and the like are elaborated upon in Section 6.

LEARNING THROUGH SERVICE FOR A NEW WORLD ORDER

With a growing interest in public and community service on the part of society as a whole and faculty and students in particular, educators and college administrators have turned to analyzing the ways in which public and community service can serve to develop our students' cognitive and problem-solving skills as well as their understanding of the world around them, through formal planned activity across the various academic disciplines. Thus service learning, a form of experiential education, has witnessed a tremendous amount of attention from faculty across most all disciplines in the higher education milieu. Yes, this renewed interest results from a sense of loss of a common social and moral vision in the United States during the last 100 or so years (O'Neil 1990).

To commence discussion on this topic of concern, a definition is in order. What specifically is service learning? According to Stanton (1990[b]; 1988):

Service learning is traditionally viewed as a particular form of experiential learning, one that emphasizes for students the accomplishment of tasks which meet human needs in combination with conscious educational growth (p. i).

Changing Students and Their Changing Needs

Why this interest in this form of experiential learning? Our student body has changed dramatically during the past decades and thus we as college faculty see a need to provide contextual learning opportunities in a way which will permit students to formulate an understanding of the content within the context of the world around them. Proponents of service learning such as Keith cite benefits including development of citizenship skills and a respect for diversity and social responsibility (1994). And second, it is a way to promote active, integrative, and motivated learning. Keith quotes Giles:

School-sponsored service stands ready for the task. At least since John Dewey, the literature on experiential learning has claimed the superiority of action-reflection and the "connected" pedagogical approaches that characterize service, over more traditional modes of classroom instruction (1991, p. 12).

Keith believes that service learning appears to facilitate reconnecting " . . . people across diversity: teachers and students, 'minority' and mainstream, service 'providers' and 'recipients'" (p. 13).

However, service learning is not without its critics. Many educators who do see a value in service learning argue that participation in civic and community-oriented projects as a formal part of an educational program hardly is sufficient as an objective unto itself. Newmann argues that participatory activities need to be identified and designed by educators with an objective to increase a student's competence to participate as a public citizen (1990). In what Newman terms "an agenda for reflection," he outlines five dimensions necessary for a student and faculty member to act upon to master a true civic education.

These are:

> . . .the necessity for decision and action in the face of pervasive uncertainty and ambiguity; the morality of public policy and personal choice; issues of strategy in setting of policy and action goals clarification of students' personal civic commitments; and finally, how to enable students and teachers to talk with one another honestly and seriously about these issues (p. 79).

And yes, Newmann sums with an insightful comment: "The educational benefits of participation are determined largely by the kinds of reflection it stimulates" (p. 76). These five dimensions are intended to drive such reflection.

Linking Theory to Practice: Cross-Disciplinary Pedagogical and Instructional Issues and Benefits

Meeting the needs of a new world order

What makes for socially responsible undergraduate education? Stanton recognizes the overlapping goals and objectives of the movements toward public service, civic education, and experiential learning (1990a). He discusses the need to clarify the benefits to be accrued to the undergraduate liberal-arts learner from such an overlapping of goals and objectives. Stanton does see a complementary benefit from close scrutiny of what has been learned from these several movements. He offers:

> *By drawing from what has been learned from these streams of work, we can establish a means of effectively integrating public and community service-based learning into the liberal-arts curriculum.*
>
> *. . .When effectively structured, facilitated, related to discipline-based theories and knowledge, and assessed, public and community service-based learning is the means for linking the initiative to develop students' social responsibility with the efforts to improve undergraduate education* (p. 186).

What better way to connect the new world order to course contents, ideas, concepts, and phenomena! It often is difficult in large course sections for students to have any direct experience with the phenomena or populations they study, according to McCluskey-Fawcett and Green (1992). Therefore, at the University of Kansas developmental-psychology students participate in community service settings for neighborhood children and their families. They gain firsthand experience about such issues as victim blaming, adolescent pregnancy, child abuse, poverty, etc. At Georgetown University, undergraduates visit the District of Columbia's prison and together with inmates study "Prison Literature" as a class for college credit. Both students and prisoners benefit, claims O'Connor:

> *Creating occasions for productive learning exchanges with community members is one way to help prisoners begin to locate a sense of non-criminal self as they engage in gaining the knowledge, skills, and emotional strength needed to contend with the prison society and later with the community beyond the walls* (1994, p. 4).

Olszewski and Bussler (1993) support Stanton's and O'Connor's arguments that a university's goal should include the development of its students' sense of both social responsibility as well as of what is learned by contributing to society. They relate that:

*In a legitimate service-learning project, there will be
ample opportunity for decision-making and for problem-solving, as well as for interpersonal skill building,
critical thinking, cooperation, and identification of
priorities and values* (p. 8).

Accordingly, goals educators strive for when using service
learning as an instructional strategy include:

- Clarification of a sense of social justice
- Opportunities to benefit from voluntary service
- Developing a student's cognitive and problem-solving
  skills
- Furthering one's academic knowledge and leadership
  abilities.

Service learning in the curriculum

We already have made the argument for experiential learning activities as a cognitive development facilitator. What
special attributes does service learning possess in the experiential education continuum? Perhaps service learning's greatest contribution is its unique ability to meet the needs of
American society for responsible civic learning. O'Neil's
concerns for revisiting the structure and methodology for
delivering what is termed a liberal civic education emerges
in part from his concern over a loss of a public moral vision
(1990). He argues:

*If the contemporary notion of the liberal arts or civic
arts turns out to be a jumble of unrelated distribution
requirements which provide at best only very narrow
technical expertise with little connection to a broader
ground of meaning, then it may be that the curriculum
reflects the moral order of the surrounding world. . .*
(p. 196).

O'Neil's concerns have centered around the conceptual and
practical relationships among undergraduate education, in
particular the liberal arts, civic education, and experiential
education. He proposes that our need to revisit these relationships stems from a changing American society — changing both in terms of technological complexity and in terms
of citizen demographics. Wade offers that "in the process of

making important contributions, students are learning academic skills and content through serving" (1994, p. 6).

And O'Neil sums:

> *Opportunities for students to participate in service-learning internships, action research, and other direct experiences of public life will be an essential component of civic renewal in the United States. Service-learning and other forms of experiential education provide vehicles for learning the basic cornerstone of civic judgment — the capacity for considered reflection on experience* (1990, p. 199).

Buchen and Fertman discuss some recent developments in the service-learning movement (1994). Nationally, the Clinton administration has provided a strong funding foundation for its growth. Clinton has created his version of the Peace Corps, known as "AmeriCorps," which provides stipends and college allowances to youth undertaking public service.

And Lashaw and Hocking discuss the Swearer Center for Public Service's approach (1994). This center, located at Brown University, was established to "assist students in connecting their intellectual development with community-based experiential learning" (p. 14). It uses college-age students as mentors for school-age children. Brown students work either with one child or a small group of children. Learners and mentors become acquainted with each other's families, customs, similarities and differences, and world perspectives. Lashaw and Hocking offer:

> *Rather than thinking narrowly of college student service as an opportunity to "give back" — a contemporary notion of noblesse oblige — active, successful mentors can make new discoveries and develop latent skills through their interactions with a learner* (p. 15).

Motivating a diverse student body
Boyer also offers that the service program should not be fundamentally career oriented (1990). Rather, it should meet the goals and needs of the learner performing the service.

A program called "SHARE" involves freshmen and sophomores in a community-based food-service program.

Boyer is quoted as stating, "These values are important in life, whether one's service is ultimately related to a career or not" (p. 105). Therefore, according to Care, it should "help students examine their ethical beliefs and their career preparation in order to integrate them in some harmonious and humanistic way" (1994, p. 6).

What does service learning within a liberal-arts program offer to the student, such that an absence of such activity would result in lessor learning outcomes? Kendall suggests that the following are "frequent results" of an effective service-learning integration into programs of study (1990[a]). Students benefit by:

- Developing a habit of critical reflection on their experiences, enabling them to learn more throughout life
- Being more curious and motivated to learn;
- Being better able to perform better service
- Strengthening their ethic of social and civic responsibility;
- Feeling more committed to addressing the underlying problems behind social issues;
- Understanding problems in a more complex way and being able to imagine alternative solutions;
- Demonstrating more sensitivity to how decisions are made and how institutional decisions affect people's lives;
- Respecting other cultures more and being better able to learn about cultural differences;
- Learning how to work more collaboratively with other people on real problems; and
- Realizing that their lives can make a difference (pp. 38-39).

Herein we see that these frequent results are complimentary to the general outcomes and goals of experiential learning for liberal-arts programs discussed in Section 2 and should be considered college creditworthy. Olszewski and Bussler describe efforts at The College of Education at Mankato State University in Minnesota. Mankato State has developed service learning into its curriculum. The program grants four credits to teacher education students who serve 40 to 50 hours in a local community agency, attend a weekly class seminar, and make site visits to communities practicing service learning in their public schools.

The culminating experience requires them to develop recommendations regarding integrating service learning into teacher preparation. The ultimate goal of such an activity is to ensure that future teachers appreciate the benefits of involvement of parents and citizens in the schools. It is anticipated that over time the efforts of teachers who see the value in integrating service learning into the general curriculum will filter down to the greater society through their teachings, making service learning an accepted practice at all grade levels.

For example, at Bronx Community College in New York City, a program called "SHARE" involves freshmen and sophomores in a community-based food-service program. The goal of the program, according to Kendall, is:

> To train [a] core group of students to organize and run a food program for students and community residents, to reduce student indebtedness by paying students through work-study, to improve academic retention. . . . [The] program supports students' intellectual, ethical, moral, career, civic, and personal development and sense of social responsibility (1990b, p. 300).

And at nearby Lehman College, also in the Bronx, students are able to participate in a community service program called the "Observer Project," which provides service to local inner-city small-business owners. Students work with neighborhood small-business owners to assist with business-development activities such as running a local newspaper for the community.

To reduce student indebtedness by paying students through work-study, to improve academic retention. . . . [The] program supports students' intellectual, ethical, moral, career, civic, and personal development and sense of social responsibility.

Administrative Issues and Concerns

Dickson suggests that faculty have a philosophical conflict with service learning as a formal instructional process, including a tendency to structure community service types of activities (for example, what he termed "the humane application of knowledge") separate and apart from the formal curriculum (1982). Stanton concurs and adds that service learning "is more of a program emphasis, representative of a set of educational, social and sometimes political values, rather than a discrete type of experiential education" (p. 65).

Perhaps the greatest concern expressed by faculty and administrators respective to service learning is how to effectively integrate this activity into their courses. Herein, Sigmon outlines three principles worth consideration:

Principle One: Those being served control the service(s) provided. Principle Two: Those being served become better able to serve and be served by their own actions. Principle Three: Those who serve also are learners and have significant control over what is expected to be learned (1990, p. 57).

With respect to administrative acceptance of service learning as an instructional strategy, an interesting finding in the literature is that among the institutions of higher education that successfully are providing opportunities to students through service learning, the community college is emerging as a specific kind of institution of higher education that is excelling in its service-learning efforts, according to Gleazer (1990). The former president of the American Association of Community and Junior Colleges offers:

Two major movements in education are merging in a manner that can produce change. One of these movements is the remolding of the two-year college into a community-based, performance-oriented, post-secondary educational institution now generally known as the community college. The second is the evolution of the student volunteer movement into the field of service-learning (p. 160).

Why are community college faculty and administrators more receptive? As a unique institution of higher education, the community college can structure service-learning activities in many different ways. Some that Gleazer offers from his experience-based vantage point include:

- The community college can serve as an umbrella organization providing service-learning opportunities for a multitude of social service kinds of activities within the community.
- A community college's facilities, inasmuch as they are publically supported, can be made available to the community at large for service-learning activities (literacy education, job training, and small-business incubators, for example).
- Faculty of the community college, as members of its community, naturally are interested in positive social change

and in their students' educations. Together these add to
service learning.

- The students of the community college are the college's
greatest resource. Through their knowledge of the community and interest in its furtherance, they are in a
unique position to provide service back to their communities as they learn in the community college (p. 161).

Service-learning program planning

Across all of higher education, though, Hofer offers administrators and faculty suggestions for designing interdisciplinary
service-learning and liberal-arts programs (1990). Citing
experiences at the University of Kentucky Office of
Experiential Education, she discusses and describes some of
the necessary components to making an interdisciplinary
offering successful. Among these are course or project offerings that are timely and practical for students.

For instance, UK offered a course titled, "Ethics and
Decision-Making in Public Service." The objective of the
program was to:

*assist students to examine the ethical basis and value
assumptions of decision making in preparation for their
future roles as professionals and as citizens* (p. 129).

As a team-taught course, students were able to participate in
full-time public-sector internships, working 30 hours per
week and earning three credits for the seminar and an additional 12 credits for specific readings. These readings were
faculty-agreed and contractually specified with the students.

Success in designing a program such as this, according to
Hofer, is faculty input — involving as many faculty across
the campus as possible. If faculty see the benefits to the
program it will work, thus mitigating any resistance to this
new form of instruction. After all, faculty must, in turn, sell it
to their students. Likewise, student input is a necessary
ingredient as well. Student word-of-mouth will market programs successfully. And, of course, community input and
support will be necessary to ensure adequate opportunities
across the community for experiential education. In UK's
case, politicians helped in the Washington, D.C., field experience. Funding is important, and the grants and contracts
people can be valuable in this regard.

These several principles are further highlighted by Boyer and should be considered when planning service programs (1990). He argues that service programs should commence with clearly stated educational objectives, and these objectives should be derived from the community-based organizations served. The support for service learning extends beyond the college — "into homes, communities, and government services" (Wade 1994). Certainly this statement is true and reflected throughout all of the experiential learning literature. And it should be! The program should be carefully introduced and promoted creatively. Planning is essential to the ultimate success of service-learning programs. The educational institution as well as the community should be the targets of the service activity. Herein, Wade suggests that activities such as mentoring, tutoring, and the like can be valuable for both the educational institution and the service learner.

EXPERIENTIAL LEARNING THROUGH COOPERATIVE EDUCATION: Linking Classroom and Community for Economic Development

As cited earlier, the rationale for college faculty and administration to attain a conceptual understanding of and appreciation for externally delivered experiential learning activities delivered through such instructional modes as cooperative education, clinicals, externships, apprenticeships, and practicums results from an increasing need to bridge the university and its business and civic communities. This need for partnerships of business and education has reached the forefront of concern among educators and entrepreneurs alike (Cantor 1990; Mosser and Muller 1990).

And according to Mosier (1990) and Moore (1994[b]) and as cited in the *Workforce 2000 Report*, during the next several decades, as the nature of the workplace changes, more workers will need retraining (hence, lifelong learning) and more adults will return to college at all levels and in all disciplines. Promoting experiential learning partnerships by colleges with business and civic communities can facilitate meeting mutual goals and objectives by providing better learning environments (more accessible, affordable, and realistic) for adult students and specifically our nontraditional students (for example, a forming of learning organizations). It also will help to maximize mutual resources and promote community economic development and, thus, business well-being.

We as faculty have a responsibility to our social and economic communities. These responsibilities include:

1. To provide business outreach and assistance (a service mission);
2. To provide realistic learning opportunities for our students (a teaching mission); and
3. To create new knowledge and information by keeping abreast of trends within our respective disciplines (a research mission).

Via links with business and community we can meet our missions and perhaps positively affect local economic development.

What is economic development? Economic development has been described as those proactive interventions within a community that provide catalytic actions to spur investment, job creation, and fuller employment (Cantor 1990). Some of these interventions can and are created by the academic community. In fact, Cayan and Jacquart cite additional benefits which are afforded the professor in one's efforts to expand the curriculum outside of the classroom — including a "helping hand" from businesspeople in the instructional process — both off and on campus — and a fresh perspective on the subject and state-of-the-art practices for the professor (1990).

And Cantor offers:

> . . . *from the economic development perspective where a new or expanding firm has requirements for entry-level workers, the availability of job training resources (for recruitment, screening, and training) makes a particular local geographical area more attractive. . . . In many cases, employers acknowledge that the availability of training assistance can be the most important factor when considering whether to expand or relocate their businesses* (1990, p. 121).

If our students are to have a "place in the sun" upon graduation, then the condition of the local economy is important to those of us in the classroom. A concise understanding of the state-of-the-art higher education partnership practices with business and industry and the community for using experiential learning education is needed.

A rationale for college involvement in economic development

College presidents — in particular, community college presidents — have demonstrated a very focused interest in academic programming to support local economic development. Beginning in the mid-1980s we have witnessed considerable activity nationally in college economic development partnerships with local communities (Cantor 1990). Kopeck states: "Community college presidents must support activities aimed at fostering environments that encourage developers to invest new money in their communities and to help existing firms grow" (1991, p. 41). Higher education can and does have a significant investment in local economic development. In fact, Kopeck cites Katsinas and Lacey, who state:

> . . . *there appear to be five major reasons that business executives are increasingly looking to community colleges for creative local responses to changing economic*

*needs: (1) recognition of the community college as a
source of assimilation assistance to new immigrants to
a region, (2) recognition of the need for new directions
to expand and diversify a given local economy in
response to the economic disruptions of the early 1980s,
(3) recognition of flaws in federal and state employment assistance and job-training policies in the larger
context of economic and demographic change, (4)
recognition of shortcomings in current American political ideology that can prevent community colleges from
rising to their full capacity in economically assisting
their service areas, and (5) recognition that community colleges (as community-based organizations) consti-
tute a delivery system already in place to provide new
programs and services* (p. 43).

The quid pro quo
Mosier cites some of the added benefits to expanding experiential education activities with business and industry from
a college president's perspective.

Among them:

A. *An entree to expanding partnerships between the college
   and business/industry.*
B. *A base for the development of a private fund-raising program.*
C. *Diversity of educational experiences and programming.
   Partnerships and networking provide the opportunity to
   integrate the world of work and the world of education.*
D. *The student has the opportunity to build a resume which
   reflects a base of work experience.*
E. *The national mission of the two-year colleges — to build
   communities - is well served.*
F. *Vintage Tom Peters — cooperative education builds the
   self-esteem of the student, the businessman and the college
   staff. Everyone wins.*
G. *In a time when time is at a premium cooperative education offers a fast track to educational achievement.*
H. *Students earn while they learn.*
I. *Cooperative education feeds the sensitivity of a college to
   its ever-changing environment.*
J. *Employers are given the opportunity to grow their own
   outstanding employees* (1990, p. 3).

Let's look at the motivators and facilitators from the stand-point of each of the major players.

Instructional Benefits to Faculty

One means of expanding experiential education delivery is through the academic institute. Worthington discusses the use of the small-business institute as a means to bring the real world to his advertising program (1992). In a small town or city, faculty cannot easily co-op with business in advertising, the small-business institute serves as a mechanism to reach small firms in need of advertising services. Here the advertising student can learn and experience real-world advertising simultaneously.

And let's not forget service learning. Raupp and Cohen add: "Student volunteerism can supplement trained professionals to ensure that the benefits of psychological knowledge and practice have direct impact on improving the human condition" (1992, p. 25). Additionally, legal-assistance centers, counseling centers, apprenticeships, etc., all are viable means by which to link higher education and the community. Baker-Loges and Duckworth extend Mosier's argument concerning the *Workforce 2000* report's findings that as we approach the next millennium, a majority of all new employment will require higher education (1991). For business and higher education the implications are clear.

Baker-Loges and Duckworth add, "Cooperative education is the only collaborative program that has a successful track record of involving business, industry, and education in joint training efforts" (p. 254).

According to Rheams and Saint, "Ongoing changes in technology, the economy, and the work force require different methods of educating and training workers" (1991, p. 47). And as cited earlier, Moore adds some thoughts about the changing images of work and work organizations that have implications for experiential education. Specifically, he argues that a healthy business and economic condition will be brought around only through a systematic redesign of the workplace. And this can be facilitated to some degree through (1) students who see firsthand how this happens and (2) educated students who bring these kinds of ideas into the workplace as change agents.

In addition to the benefits of recruitment and retention cited earlier, experiential education helps to ensure that education and training programs meet employer expectations. To make the various forms of experiential education external to the classroom more "user friendly" to employers, thus ensuring that the college's programs do, in fact, meet both student and local employer needs and expectations, Rheams and Saint cite Waddell:

> . . . (1) structure the program in such a way and make it of sufficient duration that employers are motivated to invest in training and use the program as their primary recruitment source, (2) develop co-op positions that are so substantive that highly educated adults are challenged, (3) locate the positions in curricula with great professional potential and a dearth of entry-level opportunities, and (4) earn faculty support by showing how students are recruited and retained rather than lost because of their co-op participation (1990, p. 51).

Interns are no more certain of their career choices than other, similar students before the internship but are more certain after the internship.

What are some of the forms of external experiential education available to faculty? Let's look at them.

Internships

Internships are experiential learning activities that bridge academia and the profession for students. As described in the second section, internships are used in many liberal-arts disciplines. Neapolitan's study of the effects of an internship experience on clarification of career choice demonstrates the value of this form of experiential learning (1992). He sums with:

> Interns are no more certain of their career choices than other, similar students before the internship but are more certain after the internship. Therefore it appears that the internship experience contributes significantly to clarification of career choice, particularly by providing useful career information (pp. 225-26).

What are some other disciplines using internships? Geography internships at Illinois State University allow students to engage in a full-time experiential learning activity connected to their major. Through compensated work experiences off-campus in environmental management, production or automated cartography, historical geography, or stereoplotting, students are able to "try out the world of work" and gain the necessary work skills to productively enter the profession upon graduation. This form of coordinated work experience provides an atmosphere to develop a greater sense of responsibility for the student's efforts. Illinois State University was the first Illinois college to offer such liberal-arts internships (Sublett 1989).

Experiential learning in the forms of international internships (such as in Germany, as in Weinmann's [1992] case) assist students in the sciences and engineering at Eastern Michigan University to meet these goals.

Internship configurations

Group internships are used at some colleges. These are internship opportunities that can be undertaken by multiple students with similar interests and goals. The benefits of such internships accrue both to the institution and students. Where internship opportunities are limited within a community, allowing multiples of two or more students to partake of an opportunity simultaneously maximizes the available limited resources. Additionally, students with limited abilities (language or other specific skill) can be assisted by their peers as mentors.

Sublett describes summer off-campus and full-time internships. These internships allow students to engage in uninterrupted full-time work without needing to juggle school and work schedules. The student interns get a better feel for the world of work. These internships have been in the areas of environmental management, production cartography, automated cartography, stereo-plotting, and historical geography.

And Heermann's earlier but farsighted opinions of the multifaceted benefits of experiential learning across the curriculum are alive today in the writings and discourse of contemporary educators. As he stated so eloquently as early as 1973:

> *Philosophies of education impinge upon the orientation of cooperative education, and it is critically important for . . . college educators to guard against the mistaken notion that cooperative education is a single, nondifferentiated program with one central mission. This is simply not the case. Cooperative education can be shaped and structured to fit particular missions whether it be career exploration, personal development, upgrading,*

career preparation, or programs serving the disadvan-
taged. . . . Educators . . . must evolve a new vision of
cooperative education in light of their numerous and
varied missions premised on service to a diversity of
student needs. A multifaceted cooperative education
system with the capability of adapting to a whole range
of student orientations is clearly needed (p. 14).

And Heermann further offered,

The notion that cooperative education should be limit-
ed to particular program areas (as an adjunct to voca-
tional curriculums, for example) needs rejecting so that
its important impact to the breadth of [community col-
lege] education can begin to be understood (p. 4).

For faculty, sabbaticals in which they return to their professional situations can be refreshing and mutually beneficial.
Re reports: "Indeed, the law office sabbatical may be easier
to operate and finance, since many, if not most, law firms
would welcome the advice and expertise of law professionals in their field of practice" (1995, p. 97).

Community Benefits

Why do businesses collaborate with higher education?
According to Cantor, five explanations are prominent in the
literature:

1. Organizations successfully collaborate because they
   derive mutual exchanges from each other.
2. Organizations collaborate because they are able to
   increase their access to external funds or governance
   opportunities.
3. Organizations are given mandates to collaborate.
4. Organizations collaborate because they develop formal
   agreements between each other specifying the responsibilities of each participating organization.
5. Organizations collaborate because they have conflicting
   goals, and the collaboration allows the organizations to
   mediate their conflicts in a socially approved manner
   (1990, p. 125).

Accordingly, for a business or other community-based organizations to develop a collaborative relationship with a college for experiential learning, there would need to be: (1) a quid pro quo — something to be gained by both the organization and university or college, such as potential worker talent in the form of the student; (2) sources of new funds (or other value-added benefit) to offset the internal expenses of such a collaborative activity; (3) legislation that in some way predicated the collaboration and provided some financial incentive to engage in the collaboration such as the new federal school-to-work law; (4) written agreements between higher education and the business or organization (or parent organization, as in the case of larger business organizations with local offices) which spell out the conditions of the activity; and/or (5) circumstances which necessitate collaboration to mutually better a local situation (cooperative education to mitigate poor students from dropping out of school to go to work without the necessary skills to be valuable to the employer, for example).

Cantor offers: "Collaboration between job training and economic development efforts can occur in many ways and at many levels." He continues, "A community college may offer a class to prospective small-business entrepreneurs, or a management consultant can organize a single customized job training class for an employer" (1990, p. 122). Cantor cites the National Alliance of Business as adding additional examples suitable for higher education participation:

- Using skills training as an incentive for economic development.
- Gaining hiring and training commitments from private developers receiving public assistance.
- Making education and training programs more sensitive to the changing labor needs of local firms.
- Encouraging new economic development ventures that directly involve the unemployed and hard-to-employ (1984, p. 123).

Legislative efforts have been made to foster better relationships between business and the community. Walter discusses and describes recent legislation, including the School to Work Opportunities Act of 1994 (PL. 103-239). He specifically cites Section 3 of "The Act," which stipulates:

. . . to build on and advance a range of promising school-to-work activities, such as tech-prep education, career academies, school-to-apprenticeship programs, cooperative education, youth apprenticeship, school sponsored enterprises, [and] business-education compacts . . . that can be developed into programs funded under this Act (108STAT.571) (1994, p. 88).

Within the professional and technical fields, leaders such as Walter see such legislation as fostering community-based experiential education relationships with local business and industry.

Student Benefits

As discussed previously, service learning also has a part to play in economic development. As we learn more about the benefits of compacts with the community through service learning, we can begin to make use of it as a teaching technique and as a process for improving both learning for the student and for improving the local economic conditions for business.

Specifically, Case offers:

Service-learning programs, which seek to have a positive impact on problems related to critical human needs, usually operate completely detached from, and often with uniformed suspicion of, the profit sector of the economy. In our market economy, the profit sector controls the key resources for solving social problems. Ignoring the profit sector guarantees that the social impact of service-learning programs will be minimal (1994, p. 31).

As mentioned, the concept of national service has been brought to light by the Clinton administration. It is hoped by Leeds (1994) and others that national service will foster a weaving of several of the strands of our social fabric.

New York University's department of applied psychology is working toward this goal. Some of the activity has included approximately 200 student volunteers working with neighborhood social-service agencies serving youth in Manhattan's Lower East Side and Greenwich Village communities.

This NYU AmeriCorps-Seward Park High School partnership helps the college students fund their education and helps the kids in the high school succeed academically, thus increasing graduation rates and employment possibilities. From an economic-development perspective, the key to success, according to Leeds, in having a national service program work in a local community is as follows: First, it cannot be a source of "cheap or replacement labor" for the business community. It must involve all of the social service and community based organizations in integrated planning. Furthermore, according to Leeds, "It must stretch the imaginations of all involved. . . . Experimentation and innovation that have a basis in sound theory should be encouraged, and we should attempt to follow where they lead" (p. 17). Leeds sums up with the statement that national service must draw upon the strengths of the universities to make a marked difference.

The Quid Pro Quo: Business and Industry Benefits

What's in it for corporate America? Hayman quotes a Boeing executive, who states: "If a void exists between academe and industry, this can create a situation where schools are preparing students who do not meet the needs of employers" (1993, p. 30). We previously discuss Boeing Aerospace Corp.'s efforts to cooperatively work with colleges and universities to assist in the education of tomorrow's workforce and to promote research and development in areas of corporate interest. Boeing has corporate representatives to coordinate its corporate university interchange program and interns.

The Use of Nonprofit Corporate Entities

An interesting finding in the literature is that the nonprofit educational foundation has emerged as a mechanism to foster educational partnerships with business and the community. Hightower described a program that meets many, if not all, of the five circumstances described by Cantor for collaboration (1993). The Professional Automotive Training Center, or PATC, at Shoreline Community College in Seattle is a joint venture of the Puget Sound Automotive Dealers Association and the college.

The program's goal is to provide comprehensive competency-based and career-oriented workforce training under conditions that emulate the working environment. Herein, under automotive-dealer sponsorship, students alternate quarters of academic study with quarters of on-site work at the dealership. This program has produced upwards of 100 percent placement rate for the students. A unique attribute of this program is the involvement of the Shoreline College Foundation, a 501(c)3 organization, for partial funding of the training facility, complemented by the sale of "certificates of participation" to the community under the authority of the State Board for Community and Technical Colleges. Hence, there is an investment in local economic development by both the businesses and the community.

Cross discusses a strategic cooperative Japanese corporate model for a public/private educational partnership (1993). Initially aimed at developing and enhancing cross-cultural communication through management education and training, the Japan-America Institute of Management Science demonstrates the viability of a nonprofit educational institute to catalytically foster desired educational outcomes as well as local economic development. Cross describes the goal of the institute as:

> . . . to play a significant role in fostering international goodwill by creating a multicultural educational environment which stimulates friendly curiosity about, and among, people of various nations; to develop international management education programs and activities which balance academic theory with practical application; to provide management seminars and programs which equip business personnel with new knowledge and skills in functional areas as well as in vital contemporary management issues; to provide education and research which respond to the demands of a technologically advancing, international society (p. 4).

The institute demonstrates the viability of a partnership of business and industry and its community, and higher education — the University of Hawaii's College of Business.

Small-Business Development Centers

Another way in which college educators have met the needs of their students through experiential learning opportunities is in cooperation with the college's small-business development center, described by Carmichael (1991). And earlier we cited the advertising programs at Temple University's journalism department as operating in this manner. We cited Zeuschner's internship requirements at California State University, San Luis Obispo, in which students went out into the community and provided services to local businesses and civic associations (1991).

For rural American communities in need of economic revitalization, cooperative education also provides such stimulus. Hillman cites examples of successful practices, such as partnerships of faculty and the local chambers of commerce which provide summer employment for the teacher in the field of business, followed by fall internships for their students in the very same businesses (1994). Another example is courthouse internships for rural youth to gain insights into the legal professions. These all are viable activities for rural economic development — through cooperative education partnerships. Schmitigal also encourages students to provide a service to a firm in their rural community by putting into practice their written communication skills gained in the classroom (1993).

In closing, Mosser reiterates the benefits of cooperative ventures to bridge the university with its constituent community, as it serves as an entre to expanding partnerships between the college and business and industry (1990).

EXPERIENTIAL LEARNING IN HIGHER EDUCATION: A SYNTHESIS OF SUCCESSFUL PRACTICES

I have presented the predominant issues and practices surrounding experiential learning in higher education. These issues were discussed within the context of six categories:

1. A need for educated workers and citizens who can meet the challenges of a new world economy and order.
2. An increased understanding of learning theories and cognitive development.
3. More nontraditional learners with multitudes of learning styles and needs.
4. A changing American workplace which requires people to effectively interface with each other and understand their roles as team players.
5. A necessity for higher education to more closely interface with business to promote community economic development.
6. Administrative and faculty concerns about their roles in selection and control and evaluation of the experiential learning process.

A Systematic Approach to Designing Experiential Learning Activities

Experiential learning activities should be systematically developed instructional processes which facilitate learner mastery of the concepts, ideas, practices, problems, and procedures experienced in the classroom (Branch et al. 1991). Such instructional techniques should be planned and become an integral part of a course or program (Northfield 1989; Scott et al. 1990). Hence, as one reviews the literature in experiential learning, a pattern emerges that is traceable to sound instructional design planning and development (Cantor 1990).

The model emerging from this discussion provides for experiential learning instructional and program development, supervision, administration, and evaluation. This systems model is presented from my vantage point as a professor who is concerned about my students' abilities to compete in a changing economy and society. It is hoped that some of the complexities of implementation of experiential education in any particular college course or program will become less troublesome based upon this work.

> *Experiential learning activities should be systematically developed instructional processes which facilitate learner mastery of the concepts, ideas, practices, problems, and procedures experienced in the classroom.*

Determining Your Students' Needs: What Are Appropriate Experiential Learning Activities?

The foregoing discussion highlighted the prominent arguments for incorporating and using experiential learning activities within your college classroom. Begin by first analyzing your students and their needs and then your courses and programs. Consideration should include an analysis of your learners — their best learning styles, learning dysfunctions, if any, cultural needs and variations, and present levels of content mastery. Consideration also should be given to course content requirements, professional accreditation requirements for experiential learning, materials and resources needed and available, and numbers of students to be taught. And finally, consideration for an economic necessity for higher education to more closely interface with business and industry should be made.

Through these considerations you will determine whether your present teaching practices indeed will promote development of your students as well-educated workers and citizens who can meet the challenges of a new world economy and order and your students' potential for success in a changing American workplace which requires people to effectively interface with each other and understand their roles as team players.

As indicated in the literature, first and foremost in actual program design and development is an analysis of your learner population. Experiential learning has proved to be a good practice for helping to reinforce learner mastery and thus promote successful learning for a multitude of learner groups. These include:

- The mature learner who has been away from the formal classroom environment for some time and needs the motivational uplifting acquired through contextual learning;
- The learner who needs to see and experience the value of a subject to be motivated to learn;
- The learner who has not been successful in the classroom in the past and needs the reinforcement afforded through contextual learning;
- The learner who needs more hands-on learning to succeed benefits from experiential learning activities (Kerka 1989).

Having considered one's professional role in the classroom, specifically the best ways to teach a given subject, many of us consciously debate the effectiveness of the traditional lecture, lecture-discussion, or other variations of this commonplace theme. We also look at the benefits and constraints of contextual learning outside of the classroom. We debate this matter from the standpoint of our particular student bodies.

Some of us teach very homogeneous student populations, the mainstream of America past; others of us are working with those student populations discussed herein — the new America — rich in diversity and culture. Probably most of us have mixed student populations coupled with mixed age groups, learning styles, and goals and interests. All of this adds up to a need to seriously look at experiential learning as a tool that can aid any and all students in their learning mastery process and therefore aid the instructor in successfully teaching the subject — any subject. We all seek to meet those challenges presented earlier of equipping our students with the best possible cognitive skills to meet the challenges of a new world order.

Next, you should identify the proposed experiential learning activities that are most appropriate for your course content and that meet the cognitive development needs of your particular student population. As you look at your courses of study, determine if you have fully employed contextual learning instructional techniques that capitalize upon our increasing understanding of learning theories and cognitive development. These might be classroom-based activities such as group projects, laboratories and experiments or external activities such as fieldwork or practicums. And, have you fully considered all of your students, including the nontraditional learners with multitudes of learning styles and needs?

Do you have concerns about your students' abilities to interact with people of different social and cultural backgrounds? Remember, experiential learning also helps in clarifying career choice and values. Further, it helps promote an understanding of each other and an appreciation of cultural differences. Experiential learning is wonderful for promoting the value of diversity across the college and within the classroom and brings together people of different social, ethnic, and economic classes.

Also consider the politics of experiential learning within

your institution. You might agree that modification of traditional course material to include experiential learning in such forms as small group projects, role plays, oral histories, or any number of useful action-oriented teaching strategies which engage the learner in the subject matter is very appropriate for your instruction. Oftentimes consideration of the political aspects of college institutional curriculum decision-making is necessary. Depending upon your academic governance structure, such modifications might require debate, approval, lobbying, and the like within either/or both departmental curriculum committees and collegewide committees.

Yes, all too often political constraints in academia overshadow our concerns for exciting and meaningful classroom practices to meet student learning needs (Rosenbaum et al. 1992). However, one way to be prepared to meet the challenges from within the organization to using experiential learning activities in courses and programs is to develop defendable program specifications for experiential education.

Designing Appropriate Experiential Learning Activities
Once a decision is made to include experiential learning activities in your courses, the next step in the model is to identify and design those appropriate experiential learning activities. Ask yourself why a particular activity you are considering is or can be appropriate to meet specific objectives and instructional goals. Commence by performing a review of your course or program's instructional objectives (your subject matter, for example). Decide which aspects of your course of study either can be embellished or actually instructed more effectively for the student through experiential learning. One question might include, "Can you better involve your learners in the learning process through action-oriented learning?" As we have seen, this can involve acting out literature through a play in an English-literature class or actively using a laboratory in a biological-science class. Externally, it can involve fieldwork, observations in local business or community organizations, or formal internships.

How does the activity complement the overall course of study? It is important to identify the proper role and place for all forms of experiential learning within the syllabus. Projects and other activities should be used to experience key concepts and ideas in a course. They often are used as a mechanism to bring together the content of the course into a culminating experience. Grading criteria also are important. This is best done by assigning academic weight to the activity in some manner, based upon an appropriate form of evaluation. Thorburn suggests using internship committees to develop criteria and to set such guidelines for experiential learning, including internships (1990).

Course modifications
This author certainly has had such experiences justifying course changes to reflect incorporation of experiential learning strategies and has been called to task to justify either and/or both course development or modifications to include classroom and field-based experiential learning activities. Issues within this area have included justification of trade-offs — what is the faculty member sacrificing in the content of the subject to make time available for those action-oriented activities selected to complement the remaining material? Or, what else within the curriculum must be deleted to make room for a course which is to be expanded in credit hours to encompass the experiential learning activity? Discussion has ensued about the kinds of activities that are justifiable as appropriate for a college classroom. Are oral histories researched in the community appropriate for the study of history or political science? Or community-based surveys in a sociology course? Role-plays in communications? Operating a campus radio station in speech?

Designing experiential learning activities external to the classroom
Internship placement and supervision issues such as placement, supervision, and recordkeeping are of paramount concern when making decisions about external forms of experiential learning. Oftentimes, when experiential learning takes place within the confines of the college or college classroom, supervision can be faculty, teaching assistants, or graduate students. However, when delivered externally to the classroom, there almost always will be issues of program time for faculty field supervision (Thorburn 1990). Muller discussed the issues of justification of faculty time for supervision of interns (1989). More often than not, unless there is an administrative recognition of the value of experiential learning when making program time available for field supervision, experiential learning will not work smoothly

(Thorburn 1990). And of course, the issues of liability must be addressed, per Goldstein (1990).

Placing and interviewing candidates. Methods for student selection for various forms of external experiential learning opportunities are described in the literature. In addition to other logistics concerns, the requirements of equal opportunity will apply to screening students for fieldwork positions. Waddell suggests that recruitment of at-risk students into experiential education strengthens programs by increasing retention rates and promoting economic development (1991). To exercise care in this regard, Branch et al. discuss a six-step systems approach for students to be guided through in selecting an internship (1991). From identifying career goals, environmental assessment, review of positions and developing the terms of the internship to actually doing the internship and, finally, post-internship review — these steps help to ensure meeting program goals.

Consider program length. Waddell suggests that program length and sequence are very important to overall program success. He defines co-op as a long-term, progressive experience with a minimum of two work periods (full time, part time, consecutive or alternating).

Consider your available resources. Why the issue of resources? The literature highlights the benefit of using experiential learning to embellish lean instructional and budgetary resources. In a case in which budgets have dissipated or where very limited budgets must be shared by too many faculty and diverse programs, experiential learning can bolster your available resources.

Also consider visiting your grants officer and exploring the various external funding opportunities available. The Fund for Improving Post-Secondary Education can be one possible source. At Lehman College, Enright discusses a FIPSE grant award which supported a business community and college project in which students worked with the local business community to promote entrepreneurial growth and local economic development (1989). The literature suggests that business must be equal partners with higher education in experiential learning programs that prepare workers through cooperative education. Kopeck described a rationale for college involvement in economic development which is reflected in Lehman College's Observer Project (1991).

The Observer Project at Lehman College involves students

across the various academic disciplines working with local Bronx Borough small-business people to produce a local newspaper which disseminates news of local entrepreneurial interest. The project is funded through advertisements, monies of which are used to offset publication costs. Other federal, state, private, or philanthropic sources also might exist.

Consider the issues of practicum seminar development which also are prominent in the literature. Northfield (1989) and Cromwell (1994) describe developing practicum and seminar courses so as to ensure proper reflection about experiences on the part of the students.

Likewise, Wattson offers:

A regularly scheduled class provides hands-on experience in a sponsoring organization, mandatory reading, papers, projects, opportunities to learn from the experiences of other interns, and guidance and continuity (1992, p. 430).

This class, as a teaching assignment, provides faculty with the compensation for sponsoring the internship.

Designing service-learning activities
Another issue arises: How can the community serve as an extension of the college classroom for portions of the instruction? Try to match aspects of the course of study which can be provided through educational collaboratives of business and/or community. Look for an obvious quid pro quo to be realized through college-community partnerships for some portion of your program.

Service-learning programs are developed much like any other form of experiential learning. However, points to remember, according to Lashaw and Hocking, include:

- Learners and mentors both should help to define learning goals and outcomes.
- Learning should be connected to the previous experience and learning of the participants.
- Mentors should help learners to explicitly understand learning as it is occurring.
- Expectations between mentors and learners should be explicit, mutually understood and agreed upon, and reviewed periodically.

- Concrete exhibition of learning and skills should be encouraged to positively enhance the learner's self-concept (1994, p. 24).

Service-learning programs can be effectively undertaken with a multitude of organizations, including community-service agencies which are always open to volunteers in the form of students aspiring as professionals in the social-service fields (Roebuck and Hochman 1993).

Community-based organizations can serve as a natural classroom and embellish the available instructional resources of your college. Whenever possible, to promote links for economic development it is advisable to involve learners within your local community. Through partnerships with the community, faculty have been able to provide opportunities for their students to experience a multitude of activities otherwise not possible. Dube adds:

> *Employer financial contributions are another important source of income for institutions that operate co-op programs that are effective in helping employers meet their human resource needs* (1990, p. 771).

And, you also should look to the community to ascertain where the educational program best can marry with community needs to effect experiential learning through service learning. Novak describes cooperative relationships with the National Archives to embellish learning in communication arts (1989). By participating, the community-based organization benefits from the new talents made available by your students. Programs such as AmeriCorps are worth considering. Likewise, the nonprofits and government agencies are good sources of placement opportunities (Case 1994).

Designing teacher education practicums and internships

Specific processes and procedures for systematically developing and operating quality teacher-education internships are described by Meade (1991), Paulter (1991), Joslin and Ellis (1990), and Taylor (1990). Learners must be placed in a situation whereby he or she formally observes and reflects upon the dynamics of the classroom. A mentor (master teacher) must be assigned to guide the learner's observation.

And a formal classroom seminar, attended by the teacher educator and other interns, must occur on a regular basis to help clarify what is observed and experienced and to provide for structured reflection on the part of the learner. A follow-on semester then should be devoted to practice teaching by the learner under strict, close supervision by the mentor master-teacher. The internship period should be at least one full year, compensated, and uninterrupted. Joslin and Ellis describe programs for school administrators which should be likewise structured (1990).

Designing health careers and social-work programs

Dore, Epstein, and Herreiras discussed internships which provided opportunities for social-work students to reflect upon their own talents and interests in the social-work professions (1992). Dore et al. suggest the use of performance objectives to establish a framework for developing and operating internships and clinicals in the health-careers areas (1992). The health-care areas generally have accrediting-agency guidelines for direction of experiential learning activities. These guidelines set the framework for program development.

Delivering Appropriate Experiential Learning Activities

Program delivery includes identification of placement sites, recruitment of employees, and negotiation of agreements. In the development of placement sites, establish a reason for business and the community to cooperate with the educational institution. Rheams and Saint describe successful program designs which incorporate certain ingredients (1991). They state:

> The key ingredients . . . (1) Structure the program in such a way and make it of sufficient duration that employers are motivated to invest in training and use the program as their primary recruitment source; (2) develop co-op programs that are so substantive that highly educated adults are challenged; (3) locate the positions in curricula with great professional potential and a dearth of entry-level opportunities; and (4) earn faculty support by showing how students are recruited and retained rather than lost because of their co-op participation (p. 51).

Identify potential sites. Visit each site and determine the appropriateness of each. List the benefits to accrue to and expectations of each partner (employer and college) (see Northfield 1989). Establish written agreements. There should be a written agreement listing the kinds of activities that the student will be doing as part of the placement. Make sure there is a mutual understanding of the working conditions, salary (if any), hours of work, attendance, and evaluation process. These need to be spelled out in the written agreement. And make sure limits of liability are understood (Goldstein 1990). Consider nonprofit educational foundations as a mechanism for establishing partnerships with business and industry (Portwood and Naish 1993; Hightower 1993; Cantor 1990).

Administering Experiential Learning
Part of your decisionmaking about the form or forms of activities you choose to provide for your students will involve your analysis of the organizational structure in place in your institution for such programming. Specifically, for internships and cooperative education, some colleges have centralized program administration, oftentimes located within the student-services offices. Herein, you might need to consider using these administrative services to structure your externally delivered experiential learning (practicums, internships, and clinicals, for example) — either in whole or in part.

Notwithstanding have been the ongoing debates about the appropriateness of relinquishing faculty control over the classroom learning environment when one leaves the podium! For internships and activities external to the college, concern has included identification of who within the college supervises the learner and makes grading decisions. Of course, those of us who have been using experiential learning techniques know that with adequately planned programs we do not lose control — we share responsibility for learning with the student.

Locating and marketing experiential education opportunities
Gillman discusses the art of finding an internship (1994). Third-party brokering through organizations such as the Washington Center for Internships and Academic Seminars

are discussed in terms of their ability to match students and placements nationwide.

Also, consider issues of marketing of programs. Marketing of your experiential learning programs to your students and the community is a task which must be done both internally within the college community and externally to the community at large. Parker and Keeling discuss the need to market experiential learning both to students within the college and to employers and the general community (1990). Use newsletters, college fairs, posters, college radio stations, college newspapers, and whatever else exists to get the message out. Internally, as identified by Parker and Keeling, it is important to focus attention on ensuring that the various student bodies for whom experiential learning can most benefit be targeted for aggressive marketing. This will include minority students who traditionally have not participated in internships and the like and students aspiring to enter nontraditional professions and occupational areas.

Marketing of experiential education within the institution will require justification of length of field assignments. It might necessitate the development of summer-session sections of practicums or internships to fit in with other sequentially arranged courses and programs. This also might help mitigate the faculty-load issue, whereby the costs of section offerings might be less or whereby adjunct faculty can be secured.

Evaluation of experiential learning activities, much like any other application of evaluation, should be tied to specific experiential learning program objectives.

Evaluating the Effectiveness of Experiential Learning Activities

Evaluation of experiential learning activities, much like any other application of evaluation, should be tied to specific experiential learning program objectives. Buell (1989), Kamalipour (1991), Mason (1990), Sellnow (1992), and Dore et al. (1992) discuss program assessment to document experiential learning effectiveness. Dore et al. highlight the need to continually evaluate experiential learning. The outcomes of the experiential learning activities are then assessed against these performance objectives. Cross discusses the development of assessment modules useful for this purpose. However, faculty certainly can tackle development of appropriate strategies for their own purposes using the basic guidelines in place for test development. Dore emphasizes the need to have performance objectives guide the experiential learning activity both for learner evaluation purposes and to document the effectiveness of experiential learning programs (1992).

Documenting student field activities. What is it that students will be doing? Activities, both within and external to the classroom, must be complementary to the learning objectives of the course. There must be a direct and obvious match for activities to be considered experiential learning activities. There also is an issue of award of college credit for such activities which appears to pose problems for some college faculty (Thorburn 1990). However, where clear and measurable performance objectives guide program development and administration, such concerns can be mitigated. Gorringe highlights processes for documenting experiential learning accomplishments for appropriate college credit (1989). Gorringe suggests that credit may be granted for a student's prior learning (life and work experiences) and for formal learning contexts (courses, etc.). Portfolios often are developed for life and work-experience evaluation. It also is worth mentioning at this point the issues of the kind of compensation, if any, that students will receive. The literature is pretty emphatic that students should not receive compensation for their learning experiences.

In Closing

What has been found through this review is that experiential learning should become a part of all college curricula. As we make learning relevant for the learner, more cognitive development does take place. Learners become more responsible for their own academic attainment, become more academically successful, and, in fact, enjoy learning. Therefore, we as academics become more successful as teachers as we strive to meet our own program objectives.

REFERENCES

Acosta, V. 1991. "Integrating Experiential Learning and Critical Inquiry in Health Education: A Framework for Health Professionals." Paper presented at the annual meeting of the American Educational Research Association, Chicago. ED 339 715. 32 pp.

Anthony, J. 1991. "Involvement in Learning: Its Impact on Student Outcomes." *Community/Junior College Quarterly* 15: 391-94.

Anthony, J., M. Ewing, J. Jaynes, and G. Perkus. 1990. *Engaging Psychology and History in Experiential Learning.* McKinney, Texas: Collin County Community College. ED 321 805. 28 pp.

Baker, B.K. 1994. "Beyond MacCrate: The Role of Context, Experience, Theory, and Reflection in Ecological Learning." *Arizona Law Review.* 36(2): 287-356.

Baker-Loges, S., and C. Duckworth. 1991. "Collegiate Cooperative Education: An Old Concept for Modern Education." *Journal of Studies in Technical Careers* 13(3): 253-60.

Barnett, D., and E. Bayne. 1992. *Reflection and Collaboration in the Practicum: The Mayfair Project, Monograph No. 14.* Saskatoon: Saskatchewan University. College of Education. ED 354 220. 16 pp.

Basow, R., and M. Byrne. 1993. "Internship Expectations and Learning Goals." *Journalism Educator* 47(4): 48-54. EJ 459 140.

Baxter Magolda, M. 1993. "The Development of Contextual Knowing in Graduate and Professional Education Settings." Paper presented at the annual meeting of the Association for the Study of Higher Education, Pittsburgh. ED 365 189. 29 pp.

Beales, J. 1993. "Should Schools and Companies Be Best Friends?" *Financial Executive* 9(5): 72.

Boser, J. 1990. "The Effect of a Year-Long Internship on First-Year Teaching Performance: Studying the Effectiveness of the Internship." Paper presented at the annual meeting of the Mid-South Educational Research Association, New Orleans. ED 326 520. 16 pp.

Boyer, E. 1990. "Service: Linking School to Life." In *Combining Service and Learning: A Resource Book for Community and Public Service,* vol. 1, edited by J. Kendall and Associates. Raleigh, N.C.: National Society for Internships and Experiential Education.

Branch, R.C., R. Couch, and M.A. Orey. 1991. *A Systems Approach to Selecting an Internship.* Athens: University of Georgia, Department of Instructional Technology. ED 338 137. 13 pp.

Bryan, L. 1991. "An Uncommon Internship: Exploring Options in Careers Enhanced by Foreign Language Skills." In *Acting on Priorities: A Commitment to Excellence Dimension: Languages*

'90 Report of Southern Conference on Language Teaching. ED 348 855. 12 pp.

Buchen, I., and C. Fertman. 1994. "Service-Learning and the Dilemmas of Success." *NSEE Quarterly* 20(2): 14-15+.

Buell, C. 1989. *Beyond Instrumentation: Informal Methods of Evaluating College Internships.* ED 313 765. 9 pp.

Cantor, J. 1990. "Job Training and Economic Development Initiatives: A Study of Potentially Useful Companions." *Educational Evaluation and Policy Analysis* 12(2): 121-38.

———. 1991. "Apprenticeships, Community Colleges, and the Automotive Industry." *Vocational Education Journal* 66(7): 26-29.

———. 1992. *Delivering Instruction to Adult Learners.* Toronto, Ontario, Canada: Wall & Emerson Inc. 232 pp.

———. 1992. "Apprenticeships, Business & Organized Labor, and Community Colleges: Emerging Partnerships." *Journal of Studies in Technical Careers* 14(2): 97-114.

———. 1993. *Apprenticeship and Community Colleges: Promoting Collaboration With Business, Labor and the Community for Workforce Training.* Lanham, Md.: University Press of America.

———. 1994. "Shipyard Apprenticeships and Community Colleges." *Technical and Skills Training*: 19-24.

Care, N. 1994. "Career Choice and the Service Imperative." *NSEE Quarterly* 19(4): 6-7+.

Carmichael, J. 1991. "Meeting Small Business Needs Through Small Business Development Centers." In *Economic and Work Force Development*, edited by G. Waddell. New Directions for Community Colleges. San Francisco: Jossey-Bass.

Case, J. 1994. "The Market Economy, Community Service, and Global Citizenship." *NSEE Quarterly* 20(2): 31.

Catelli, L.A. 1995. "Action Research and Collaborative Inquiry in a School-University Partnership." *Action in Teacher Education* 16(4): 25-38.

Cayan, S., and J. Jacquart. 1990. "Internships: Lending a Hand." *ACU-I-Bulletin* 58(6): 22-24. ED 347 866.

Cheslik, F. 1989. "Professional Internships: The Use of a Valuable Learning Experience." Paper presented at the annual meeting of the International Communication Association, San Francisco. ED 316 889. 29 pp.

Clements, A.D. 1995. "Experiential-Learning Activities in Undergraduate Developmental Psychology." *Teaching of Psychology* 22(2): 115-18.

Cromwell, L. 1994. "An Internship Seminar: Integrating the

Academic and Professional Worlds." *NSEE Quarterly* 20(2): 8-9+.

Cross, K. 1994a. "The Coming of Age of Experiential Education." *NSEE Quarterly* 19(4): 1+.

———. 1994b. "The Coming of Age of Experiential Education: Part II." *NSEE Quarterly* 19(4): 8-9+.

Cross, L. 1993. "Educational Leadership: A Strategic Cooperative Japanese Corporate Model." *Leadership & Organization Development Journal* 14(3): 4-6.

Cutt, J., and M.K. Loken. 1995. "The Nature of Evidence in Assessing Cooperative Education." *Journal of Cooperative Education* 30(3): 24-38.

Deal, N., and J. Beaver. 1989. "The Missing Link: Internships in Professional Writing Programs." Paper presented at the annual meeting of the Eastern Educational Research Association, Savannah, Ga. ED 302 855. 12 pp.

Dickson, A. 1982. "A Service-Learning Retrospective." *Synergist*: 40-41.

Dore, M., B. Epstein, and C. Herrerias. 1992. "Evaluating Students' Micro Practice Field Performance: Do Universal Learning Objectives Exist?" *Journal of Social Work Education* 28(3): 353-62. EJ 457 785.

Dube, P. 1990. "Cooperative Education: A Resource for Human and Economic Development." *Journal of Chemical Education* 67(9): 771-73.

Ellis, B. 1992. "A Case Study of a Student-Run Advertising/Public Relations Agency: The Oregon State University Experience." Paper presented at the annual meeting of the Association for Education in Journalism and Mass Communication, Montreal, Quebec, Canada. ED 350 631. 15 pp.

Enright, J., and H. Crawford. 1989. "Revitalization of the Bronx: College and Merchants Collaborate." NSIEE Experiential Education 14(5): 8+.

Feeney, J., and J. Morris. 1994. "Student-Initiated Experiential Education." *NSEE Quarterly* 20(1): 14-15+.

Gardner, P., and S. Kozlowski. 1993. Learning the Ropes! Co-Ops Do it Faster. East Lansing: Collegiate Employment Research Institute, Michigan State University. ED 367 937. 18 pp.

Gettys, C. 1990. "Internship Paved the Way for First Year Positions." Paper presented at the annual meeting of the Mid-South Educational Research Association, New Orleans. ED 326 523. 18 pp.

Gillman, L. 1994. "Finding an Internship: The Value of Third-Party Brokering." *NSEE Quarterly* 19(4): 10-11.

Givelber, D.B., B. Baker, J. McDevitt, and R. Miliano. 1995. "Learning Through Work: An Empirical Study of Legal Internship." *Journal of Legal Education* 45(1): 1-48.

Gleazer, E. 1990. "Emergence of the Community College as a Center for Service-Learning." In *Combining Service and Learning: A Resource Book for Community and Public Service*, vol. 1, edited by J. Kendall and Associates. Raleigh, N.C.: National Society for Internships and Experiential Education.

Goldstein, M. 1990. "Legal Issues in Combining Service and Learning." In *Combining Service and Learning: A Resource Book for Community and Public Service*, vol. 1, edited by J. Kendall and Associates. Raleigh, N.C.: National Society for Internships and Experiential Education.

Gorringe, R. 1989. Accreditation of Prior Learning Experiences: Developments in Britain and Lessons from the USA. Blagdon, England. ED 342 318. 47 pp.

Greenberg, J.D. 1995. "Active Learning - Active Teaching: How Do You Get There From Here? *NSEE Quarterly* 20(3): 4-5+.

Gregory, S. 1990. *Does Co-Op Really Make a Difference? A Look at Graduation and Retention.* E32367. 20 pp.

Hayden, B. 1992. "Developing International Student Internships." Paper presented at the annual Eastern Michigan University Conference on Languages and Communication for World Business and the Professions, Ypsilanti, Mich. ED 347 911. 14 pp.

Hayman, E. 1993. "A Meeting of the Minds at Boeing." *Management Accounting*: 30-32.

Heermann, B. 1973. *Cooperative Education in Community Colleges.* San Francisco: Jossey-Bass.

Heinemann, H., and J.W. Wilson. 1995. "Developing a Taxonomy of Institutional Sponsored Work Experience." *Journal of Cooperative Education* 30(2): 46-55.

Herdendorf, P. 1991. "Principles of International Business: An Experiential Learning Course." Paper presented at the annual Eastern Michigan University Conference on Languages and Communication for World Business and the Professions, Ypsilanti, Mich. E34765. 11 pp.

Hightower, C. 1993. "The Partnership for Today That Works for Tomorrow: The Professional Automotive Training Center at Shoreline Community College." Paper presented at the annual convention of the American Association of Community Colleges, Seattle. E35833. 13 pp.

Hillman, C. 1994. "A Path to Rural Regeneration." *NSEE Quarterly* 19(4): 16-17+.

Hoberman, S. 1994. "Time-Honored or Timeworn?" *Journal of Vocational Education* 69(3): 28-31.

Hofer, B. 1990. "Service-Learning and the Liberal Arts: Designing an Interdisciplinary Program." In *Combining Service and Learning: A Resource Book for Community and Public Service*, vol. II, edited by J. Kendall and Associates. Raleigh, N.C.: National Society for Internships and Experiential Education.

Johnson, R. 1994. "Internships and Reverse-Internships." *NSEE Quarterly* 20(1): 3.

Joslin, A., and N. Ellis. 1990. *Merging Leadership Theories and the World of Practice; Shared Responsibility for a Successful Internship.* E32986. 25 pp.

Kamalipour, Y. 1991. "Methods of Assessing Internship Performance." Paper presented at the annual meeting of the Central States Communication Association, Chicago. ED 336 803. 18 pp.

Keith, N. 1994. "Educating Tomorrow's Citizens Through Service-Learning." *NSEE Quarterly* 20(1): 12-13+.

Kendall, J., and Associates. 1990[a]. *Combining Service and Learning: A Resource Book for Community and Public Service*, vol. 1. Raleigh, N.C.: National Society for Internships and Experiential Education. 693 pp.

————. 1990[b]. *Combining Service and Learning: A Resource Book for Community and Public Service*, vol. II. Raleigh, N.C.: National Society for Internships and Experiential Education. ED 327 120. 528 pp.

Kendall, J., J. Duley, T. Little, J. Permaul, and S. Rubin. 1986. *Strengthening Experiential Education Within Your Institution.* Raleigh, N.C.: National Society for Internships and Experiential Education.

Kerka, S. 1989. *Cooperative Education: Characteristics and Effectiveness.* ERIC Digest No. 91. Columbus, Ohio: ERIC Clearinghouse on Adult, Career, and Vocational Education. E31455. 4 pp.

Kopeck, R.J. 1991. "Assuming a Leadership Role in Community Economic Development." In *Economic and Work Force Development*, edited by G. Waddell. New Directions for Community Colleges. San Francisco: Jossey-Bass.

Lankard, B. 1991. "Tech Prep: Digest No. 108." Columbus, Ohio: ERIC Clearinghouse on Adult, Career, and Vocational Education. Center for Education and Training for Employment, The Ohio State University.

Lashaw, A., and P. Hocking. 1994. "Learners and Mentors." *NSEE*

Quarterly 19(4): 14-15+.

Laws, P.W., P.J. Rosborough, and F.J. Poodry. 1995. *New Directions for Teaching and Learning* 61: 77-87.

Leeds, J. 1994. "National Service: The Challenge." *NSEE Quarterly* 20(1): 16-17.

Linn, P. 1993. "Theory into Practice: The Role of Work in the Undergraduate Psychology Curriculum." Paper presented at the biannual meeting of the Society for Research in Child Development, New Orleans. ED 360 899. 17 pp.

Lurie, E.E., and B. Ovrebo. 1995. "Using a Cooperative Classroom Climate and Experiential Learning in Teaching Evaluation Research." *Teaching Sociology* 23(3): 252-58.

MacIsaac, D. 1990. *Teacher Induction Partnerships Program.* University of Northern Colorado, Greeley. E32124. 12 pp.

McCluskey-Fawcett, K., and P. Green. 1992. "Using Community Service to Teach Developmental Psychology." *Teaching-of-Psychology* 19(3): 150-52. E46290.

Marra, J. 1990. "A Necessary Course for the 1990s: The Student-Run Advertising Agency." Paper presented at the annual meeting of the Association for Education in Journalism and Mass Communication, Minneapolis. ED 324 709. 24 pp.

Mason, G. 1990. "Assessing Internships as Experiential Learning: The Views of Interns, On-Site Supervisors, and Intern Coordinators." Paper presented at the annual meeting of the Speech Communication Association, Chicago. ED 327 887. 25 pp.

Matson, L.C., and R. Matson. 1995. "Changing Times in Higher Education: An Empirical Look at Cooperative Education and Liberal Arts Faculty." *Journal of Cooperative Education* 30(3): 13-24.

Meade, E. 1991. "Reshaping the Clinical Phase of Teacher Preparation." *Phi Delta Kappan* 72(9): 666-69.

Megargee, E. 1990. *A Guide to Obtaining a Psychology Internship.* Muncie, Ind.: Accelerated Development Inc. ED 345 135. 210 pp.

Moore, D. 1990. "Experiential Education as Critical Discourse." In *Combining Service and Learning: A Resource Book for Community and Public Service*, vol. 1, edited by J. Kendall and Associates. Raleigh, N.C.: National Society for Internships and Experiential Education.

———. 1994. "Changing Images of Work and Work Organizations: Implications for Experiential Education — Part I." *NSEE Quarterly* 20(1): 1+.

————. 1994. "Changing Images of Work and Work Organizations: Implications for Experiential Education — Part II." *NSEE Quarterly* 20(2): 6-7+.

Mosier, R.H. 1990. "A President's View of Cooperative Education." Paper presented at the annual conference of the Cooperative Education Association, San Antonio, Texas. ED 317 853. 4 pp.

Mosser, J. 1989. *Field Experience as a Method of Enhancing Student Learning and Cognitive Development in the Liberal Arts.* ED 315 024. 20 pp.

Mosser, J., and B. Muller 1990. *Raising America's Awareness of Cooperative Education: A Historical Overview of the National Commission for Cooperative Education Public Service Advertising Campaign.* ED 314 595. 20 pp.

Mosser, J., and P. Rea. 1990. "Marketing Cooperative Education. A Workshop." Paper presented at the annual conference of the Midwest Cooperative Education Association, Grand Rapids, Mich. ED 325 646. 64 pp.

Muldoon Jr., J.P., and C.J. Myrick. 1995. "The Model United Nations: 50+ and Growing Strong." *Educational Leadership.* 53(2): 98-99.

Muller, W. 1989. *College Internship Program American Association of State Colleges and Universities.* ED 316 090. 25 pp.

————. 1990. Proceedings: The National Institute on the Assessment of Experiential Learning. Princeton, N.J.: Council for Adult and Experiential Learning. ED 339 723. 42 pp.

National Commission on Higher Education. n.d. "Developing a Comprehensive Cooperative Education Program." Boston.

Neapolitan, J. 1992. "The Internship Experience and Clarification of Career Choice." *Teaching Sociology* 20(3): 222-31. EJ 458 422.

Newmann, F. 1990. "Reflective Civic Participation." In *Combining Service and Learning: A Resource Book for Community and Public Service*, vol. 1, edited by J. Kendall and Associates. Raleigh, N.C.: National Society for Internships and Experiential Education.

Northfield, J. 1989. "Constructing the Practicum Experience." Paper presented at the annual meeting of the American Educational Research Association, San Francisco.ED 308 181. 21 pp.

Novak, D. 1992. "Communication Training for the Real World: Linking Community Needs to the Undergraduate Course." Paper presented at the annual meeting of the Speech Communication Association, Chicago. ED 354 552. 28 pp.

Novak, G. 1989. "Turning History into a Radio Program: Broadcast Interns and the National Archives." Paper presented at the annual meeting of the Speech Communication Association, San

Francisco. ED 312 715. 52 pp.

O'Brien, E. 1993. *Outside the Classroom: Students as Employees, Volunteers, and Interns.* Washington, D.C.: American Council on Education. ED 357 672. 114 pp.

O'Connor, P. 1994. "Reaching Out – Reaching in: Learning in a Maximum Security Prison." *NSEE Quarterly* 20(2): 4-5+.

Olszewski, W., and D. Bussler. 1993. "Learning to Serve – Serving to Learn." Mankato, Minn.: Mankato State University. ED 367 615. 12 pp.

Oludaja, B. 1993. "Experiential Approach to Intercultural Communication." Paper presented at the annual convention of the Southern States Communication Association and the Central States Communication Association, Lexington, Ky. ED 361 762. 13 pp.

O'Neil, E. 1990. "The Liberal Tradition of Civic Education." In *Combining Service and Learning: A Resource Book for Community and Public Service*, vol. 1, edited by J. Kendall and Associates. Raleigh, N.C.: National Society for Internships and Experiential Education.

O'Neill, M. 1992. "Undergraduate Internships: Oxymoron or Necessity?" Paper presented at the annual convention of the American Psychology Association, Washington, D.C. ED 354 456. 14 pp.

Parker, L., and A. Keeling. 1990. "Marketing Cooperative Education Programs to Multi-Ethnic Students." *Cooperative Education Marketing Digest*, No. 3. Kalamazoo, Wis.: Cooperative Education Marketing Inc. ED 319 902. 9 pp.

Parnell, D. 1996. "Cerebral Context." *Vocational Education Journal* 71(3): 18-21+.

Paull, R.C., C.Z. McGrevin, J.D. Bowick, T.R. Cannings, H.W. Hughes, and J. Schmieder. 1995. *Preparing Administrators to Meet the Challenges of a Multi-Cultural Society.* Culver City, Calif.: Pepperdine University Graduate School of Education and Psychology. ED 387 902. 15 pp.

Paulter, A. 1990. "A Review of UCEA Member Institutions Clinical Experiences/Internship/Field Experiences for Educational Leaders." Paper presented at the annual meeting of the University Council for Educational Administration, Pittsburgh. ED 331 172. 23 pp.

———. 1991. *Structured Clinical Experiences for the Preparation of Educational Leadership Personnel for the Future.* ED 331 173. 25 pp.

Polirstok, S.R. 1996. "Cultural Diversity and Learning Styles."

Lehman College Prism: 2+.

Portwood, D., and J. Naish. 1993. *Work-Based Learning and Higher Education in the USA*. London, England: Middlesex University. ED 369 316. 44 pp.

Raupp, C., and D. Cohen. 1992. "A Thousand Points of Light Illuminate the Psychology Curriculum: Volunteering as a Learning Experience." *Teaching of Psychology* 19(1): 25-30.

Re, E.D. 1995. "Law Office Sabbaticals for Law Professors." *Journal of Legal Education* 45(1): 95-98.

Rheams, P., and F. Saint. 1991. "Renovating Cooperative Education Programs." In *Economic and Work Force Development*, by G. Waddell. New Directions for Community Colleges. San Francisco: Jossey-Bass.

Roebuck, D., and A. Hochman. 1993. "Community Service Agencies and Social Studies: A New Partnership." *Social Education* 57(2): 76-77.

Rolls, J. 1992. "Experiential Learning as an Adjunct to the Basic Course: Assessment of a Pedagogical Model." Paper presented at the annual meeting of the Speech Communication Association, Chicago. ED 352 686. 22 pp.

Rosenbaum, J.E. 1992. "Guidelines for Effective School-Employer Linkages for Apprenticeship." In *Youth Apprenticeship in America: Guidelines for Building an Effective System. A Monograph: Youth and America's Future*. Washington, D.C.: William T. Grant Foundation, Commission on Work, Family, and Citizenship. ED 355 340. 82 pp.

Ross, R. 1990. "Building a Relationship With the Agency Supervisor: An Academic Internship Coordinator's Perspective." Paper presented at the annual meeting of the Speech Communication Association, Chicago. ED 330 013. 13 pp.

Russell, T. 1993. "Reflection-in-Action and the Development of Professional Expertise." *Teacher Education Quarterly* 20(1): 51-62. EJ 460 498.

Saltmarsh, J. 1992. "John Dewey and the Future of Cooperative Education." *Journal of Cooperative Education* 28(1): 6-16. EJ 462 013.

Schmidt, W., G.H. Gardner, J.B. Benjamin, R.N. Conaway, and W.A. Haskins. 1992. "Teaching the College Course Series: Directing Independent Studies and Internships in Communication." Short course presented at the annual meeting of the Speech Communication Association, Chicago. ED 353 616. 91 pp.

Schmitigal, L. 1993. "The Business Writing Agenda, Part I: Collaboration Between Business and the Undergraduate

Student." Paper presented at the annual meeting of the Conference on College Composition and Communication, San Diego. ED 361 693. 28 pp.

Seibert, J., and B. Davenport-Sypher. 1989. "The Importance of Internship Experiences to Undergraduate Communication Students." Paper presented at the annual meeting of the Speech Communication Association, San Francisco. ED 315 826. 25 pp.

Sellnow, T.L., R.S. Littlefield, and D.D. Sellnow. 1992. "Evaluating Internships and Overcoming Program Concerns and Constraints." Paper presented at the 78th annual meeting of the Speech Communication Association, Chicago. 25 pp.

Shaver, L.D., and P.M. Shaver. 1995. "Implementing Experiential Learning in the Higher Education Intercultural Communication Class." Paper presented at the annual meeting of the Southern States Communication Association, New Orleans. ED 386 770. 39 pp.

Sigmon, R. 1990. "Service-Learning: Three Principles." In *Combining Service and Learning: A Resource Book for Community and Public Service*, vol. 1, edited by J. Kendall and Associates. Raleigh, N.C.: National Society for Internships and Experiential Education.

Smythe, O. 1990. "Practical Experience and the Liberal Arts: A Philosophical Perspective." In *Combining Service and Learning: A Resource Book for Community and Public Service*, vol. 1, edited by J. Kendall and Associates. Raleigh, N.C.: National Society for Internships and Experiential Education.

Soter, T. 1993. "A Business Plan for Education." *Management Review* 82(9): 10-16.

Stanton, T. 1988. *Service Learning: An Annotated Bibliography: Linking Public Service With the Curriculum.* Raleigh, N.C.: National Society for Internships and Experiential Education.

———. 1990[a]. "Liberal Arts, Experiential Learning and Public Service: Necessary Ingredients for Socially Responsible Undergraduate Education." In *Combining Service and Learning: A Resource Book for Community and Public Service*, vol. 1, edited by J. Kendall and Associates. Raleigh, N.C.: National Society for Internships and Experiential Education.

———. 1990[b]. "Service Learning: Groping Toward a Definition." In *Combining Service and Learning: A Resource Book for Community and Public Service*, vol. 1, edited by J. Kendall and Associates. Raleigh, N.C.: National Society for Internships and Experiential Education.

Stone, J., and R. Wonser. 1990. "Alternative Strategies for Providing

Work Experience." St. Paul: University of Minnesota; Minnesota
Research and Development Center for Teacher Education. ED
323 325. 55 pp.

Stoner, M. 1989. *Internship Handbook and Policy Statement.* Mount
Vernon, Ohio: Mount Vernon Nazarene College. ED 306 783.
45 pp.

Stross, J.K. 1995 "Implementation and Evaluation of a Primary Care
Preceptorship." *Academic Medicine* 70(3): 202-04.

Sublett, M. 1989. "Geography Internships: First, the Good News."
Paper presented at the annual meeting of the Association of
American Geographers, Baltimore. ED 310 985. 12 pp.

Taylor, N., A. Samaras, and A. Gay. 1994. "Making Connections:
Aligning Theory and Field Practice." Paper presented at the
annual meeting of the American Association of American
Colleges for Teacher Education, Chicago. ED 367 597. 24 pp.

Taylor, T. 1990. "Public Relations Guidelines for Cooperative
Education." *Cooperative Education Marketing Digest,* Series 6.
Kalamazoo, Wis.: Cooperative Education Marketing Inc. ED 323
363. 9 pp.

Thompsen, P.A. 1991. "Enhancing the Electronic Sandbox: A Plan
for Improving the Educational Value of Student-Operated Radio
Stations." Paper presented at the annual meeting of the
Broadcast Education Association, Las Vegas. ED 339 055. 10 pp.

Thorburn, N. 1990. "Enriching the Liberal Arts: Integrating
Experiential Learning Throughout a Liberal Arts College." In
*Combining Service and Learning: A Resource Book for
Community and Public Service,* vol. 1, edited by J. Kendall and
Associates. Raleigh, N.C.: National Society for Internships and
Experiential Education.

Vickers, N. 1990. A *Comparison of the Starting Pay of Cooperative
Education Graduates With That of Non-Cooperative Education
Graduates.* Drury College: Capstone Seminar Paper. ED 349 455.
51 pp.

Waddell, G. 1991. "Economic and Work Force Development." In
New Directions for Community Colleges, edited by Cohen and
Brawer. San Francisco: Jossey-Bass, Inc.

Wade, R. 1994. "A Century of Service-Learning: Can We Get There
From Here?" *NSEE Quarterly* 20(1): 6-7+.

Wagner, R., D. Scharinger, and J. Sisak. 1992. "Enhancing Teaching
Effectiveness Using Experiential Techniques: Model
Development and Empirical Evaluation." Paper presented at the
annual meeting of the Midwest Region of the Academy of
Management, St. Charles, Ill. ED 345 908. 10 pp.

————. 1995. "Enhancing Teaching Effectiveness Using Experiential Techniques: Model Development and Empirical Evaluation." Paper presented to the Midwest Region of the Academy of Management, St. Charles, Ill. ED 345 908. 10 pp.

Walter, R. 1994. "At Issue: The Rebirth of Cooperative Education." *Journal of Industrial Teacher Education* 32(1): 86-89.

Washington, W. 1992. *Cooperative Education: Training Health Managers.* Los Angeles: ERIC Monograph. ED 347 326. 12 pp.

Wattson, K.W. 1992. "An Integration of Values: Teaching the Internship Course in a Liberal Arts Environment." *Communication Education* 41(4): 29-39.

Weinmann, S. 1992. "Internships in Germany: Unique Opportunities for Students of Science and Engineering." Paper presented at the annual Eastern Michigan University Conference on Languages and Communication for World Business and the Professions, Ypsilanti, Mich. ED 347 848. 13 pp.

Worthington, B. 1992. "Bringing the 'Real World' Into the Advertising Classroom." Paper presented at the annual meeting of the Association for Education in Journalism and Mass Communication, Montreal, Quebec, Canada. ED 349 602. 9 pp.

Zeuschner, R. 1991. "Learn by Doing: Practical Applications on and Off Campus." Paper presented at the annual meeting of the Speech Communication Association, Atlanta. ED 344 267. 10 pp.

INDEX

A

academic programs and employers, increasing importance of link between, x

Academic Seminars, 88-89

Acosta (1991)
benefits and issues of experiential learning in professional preparation programs, 47

active learning as central concept, 20

active-learning strategies
key ingredients in constructing effective, 21

active teacher
interested in student learning through thinking and solving complex problems, 23
role in structuring complex academic tasks, 21

administering experiential learning, 88

administrative issues and concerns, 15-17

"advanced skills" articulation model
Tech Prep as an, 54

"agenda for reflection", 58

"aidship", 45

Albion College, 30

AmeriCorps, 61
teaching value of programs such as, 86

Anthony (1991)
benefits of learning in terms of impact on student's outcomes, 50

Anthony et al. (1990)
describes active learning approaches, 23-24

Antioch College in Ohio
contextual approach to teaching psychology at, 24-25

apprenticeship
major features, 52-53
method to deliver quality education and training, as a, 52
movement toward experiential learning for structured work force, as a, 52

Auburn University, 47

automotive manufactures
collaborative agreements between community colleges and, 53

B

Baker (1994)
theory of ecological learning, 42

Basker-Loges and Duckworth (1991)

"career development"
as primary objective of experiential education through
cooperative education, 32
Carmichael (1991) describes cooperation with college's small-
business development center to meet experiential learning
opportunities needs, 77-78
Carnegie Task Force on Teaching as a Profession, 39
Catelli (1995)
inquiry made 'critical' by participants of engaging in rigorous
questioning, 5
professional teacher preparation requires "reflection-in-action",
41
Catholic University, 40-41
"center" as an active-learning ingredient, 33-34
Chrysler
collaborative agreements between community colleges and, 53
Clements (1992) citation of Stevens and Richards definition of
Experiential education, 1
Clements (1995)
experiences perceived selectively by ignoring inconsistent
information, 25
"climate" construct of Greenberg, 26-27
clinical experiences
Health Care documents that experiential education is often
required through, 47
cognitive development
experiential learning promotes, 8
further insights into the relationships with experiential learning, 7
outcomes, 23
service learning as facilitator of, 60
through experiential learning is described as happening
through a continuum, 42
cognitive psychology research
suggests experiential education has built into it many
pedagogical advantages, 6
College of Education at Mankato State University in Minnesota, 62
college retention rates improved as a result of involvement in
experiential learning, 9
college student
increasing average age of, 27
instinctively recognize the value of experiential education,
29
Collegiate Employment Research Institute, 50

immersing students in an activity and then asking for their
    reflection on it, 1
in professional areas such as health and education, 2
in the arts and humanities, 2
in the physical sciences and mathematics, 2
in the social and behavioral sciences, 2
number of institutions offering, 3
experiential educational experiences
    findings of study on value of, 50
experiential learning
    as a process of learning and a method of instruction, 1
        as a process to ensure integration of such values, 22
        incompatibility with more traditional learning, 19
    intentions of this review of the literature on, 1
    predominant issues and practices in higher education, 79
        reasons for increased interest in, ix
    reason for need for, 33
experiential learning activities
    difficulties in implementation of, 33
    what are appropriate, 80-82
experiential learning and psychology
    commentary on the match of, 28

F

factors that complicate use and institutionalization
    of experiential learning activities into the curriculum, 15
faculty responsibility to social and economic communities, 67
Feeney and Morris (1994)
    formal experiential education may be shunned by some faculty,
        15
field experience
    as necessary part of curriculum, 34
FIPSE.   See Fund for Improving Post-Secondary Education
five principal features of
    contextualist view of situated, functionally engaged cognition, 42
Ford Motor Co. collaborative agreement with Middlesex County
        College New Jersey, 52
foreign-languages
        educators use of experiential learning in their programs, 30
        adaptation of experiential learning enhancing traditional
        classroom learning, 22
formal experiential education may be shunned by some faculty, 15

framework for clinical experience development
    based upon five goals, 43
"frequent results" of service-learning integration into programs of
    study, 62
Fund for Improving Post-Secondary Education, 84

G

Gardner and Kozlowski (1993)
    findings of study on value of experiential educational
        experiences, 50
Gardner's (1990) leadership theories, 45
General Motors
    collaborative agreements between community colleges and, 53
geography
    adoption of experiential learning to enhance traditional
        classroom learning, 22
    internships, 71
Georgetown University, 59
Gettys (1990)
    case study of five-year teacher education programs described
        by, 39-40
Giles (1991)
    service learning value, 57
Gillman (1994)
    discusses the art of finding an internship, 88
Givelber et al. (1995)
    impact of contextualist insights on legal pedagogy, 37
Goldstein (1990)
    legal issues that must be recognized by the university, 34
Gorringe (1989)
    highlights processes for documenting experiential learning
        accomplishments, 90
Greenberg (1995)
    active learning as central concept, 20
Gregory (1990)
    students enter graduate school at increased rate after
        experiential learning, 10
group internships, 72

H

Hayman (1993)
    business perspective of experiential learning in the sciences and
        engineering, 49

health-career areas
    use of performance objectives in, 87
Health Care accepts and often requires experiential education as
        clinical experiences, 47
health professions experiential education
    utility of process for undergraduate students in, 47-48
Heermann (1973) on cooperative education
        not a single, non differentiated program, 72
    "career development" as objective of experiential education
        through, 32
Heinemann and Wilson (1995), 3
    Most faculty rely upon a didactic approach to instruction, 4
"helping hand" benefit from business people, 68
Herdendorf (1991) use of individualized learning contracts, 22
high-level cognitive learning outcomes techniques
    less-structured cooperative more effective than traditional
        individualistic, 25
Hillman (1994)
    cooperative education as stimulus for economic revitalization, 78
history
    active learning approaches in, 23
history program at Collin Country Community College
    included experientially based work in the forms of video project
        requirements, 25
Hoberman (1994) on jobs
    large employers account for relatively few post secondary
        cooperative education, 3-4
Hofer (1990)
    suggestions for interdisciplinary service-learning and liberal-arts
        programs, 65
Holmes plan as philosophical underpinning of five-year program, 40
Holmes Report, 38
Honda
    collaborative agreements between community colleges and, 53
"Human Corps", 29

I
Illinois State University, 71-72
importance of active vs. passive learning, 7
intentions of this review of the literature on experiential learning, 1
interdisciplinary service-learning and liberal-arts programs
    suggestions for designing, 65
international internships, 72

internship committees
    use to develop criteria, 83
internships
    art of finding an, 88
        restricted to best students in programs, 16
    use of, 71-72
intrinsic value of experiential learning in higher education, 20-21
issues and practices in higher education surrounding experiential
        learning, 79

J

Japan-America Institute of Management Science, 77
Japanese corporate model for public/private educational
        partnership, 77
Johnson (1994)
    need broader understanding of the purposes of education and
        best ways to teach, 26
Joslin and Ellis (1990)
    description of school administrator preparation program, 45
    specific processes for developing teacher-education internships,
        86
Junior Achievement of Central Indiana, 46
justification
        of course changes to reflect incorporation of experiential
        learning strategies, 83
        of faculty time for supervision of interns, 83

K

Kamalipour (1991) discuss
    program assessment to document experiential learning
        effectiveness, 89-90
Keith (1994)
    service learning benefits, 57
Kendall (1990a) suggests
    "frequent results" of service-learning integration into programs
        of study, 62
Kiser (1991)
    basic courses are theoretically oriented, and devote less time to
        developing skills, 27
Kolb's Theory, 7
    application to meet Mosser's (1989) cognitive development
        outcomes, 23
Kopeck (1991)

community colleges support activities encouraging investment of new money, 68

rationale for college involvement in economic development, 84

L

Lankard (1991)

Tech Prep as an "advanced skills" articulation model, 54

Lashaw and Hocking discuss (1994)

Swearer Center for Public Service approach, 61

law office sabbatical

as easier to operate and finance, 73

Laws, Rosborough, and Poodry (1995)

activity based curricula facilitates the development of scientific reasoning, 5

discuss value of experiential learning in teaching of introductory physics, 49

lawyering has its genesis in experiential learning, 37

"lead schools"

call for, 39

"Learn and Serve America: Higher Education Program", 27

learner

groups that profit from experiential learning, 80

population analysis is first step in program design and development, 80

learning is incomplete without application, generalization and experimentation, 20

learning organizations

modern economic and social organizations need to be, 13

learning process

greater effort results in greater achievement in, 50

legal issues that must be recognized by the university, 34

Lehman College in the Bronx, 54, 63, 84

Observer Project, 84-85

liability of acts of the student, 34

liberal arts

education goals, 19

experiential learning yet to establish itself as fully respectable in, 36

program needs to be successful in meeting student career goals, 32

students, broad goals for, 26

liberal civic education

concerns for delivering a, 60

Linn (1993)
   contextual approach to teaching psychology at Antioch College
      in Ohio, 24-25
Locker (1986)
   learning is incomplete without application, generalization and
      experimentation, 20
Lurie and Overbo (1995)
   evaluation research course as experiential learning, 11

M

McCluskey-Fawcett and Green (1992)
   difficult for large course section students to experience what
      they study, 59
MacIsaac (1990) description of a
   teacher induction partnership program at University of Northern
      Colorado, 43-44
Magolda (1993)
      assess student feelings on experiential learning to develop
         contextual learning, 49
   five major themes in developing contextual knowledge, 42
Mankato State University in Minnesota, 62
marketing experiential learning programs, 89
      to minority or nontraditional student populations as an
         issue, 16
Mason (1990) discuss
   program assessment to document experiential learning
      effectiveness, 89-90
Matson and Matson (1995)
   students demanding relevance in their education, especially
      within the liberal arts, 4
Meade (1991)
   clinical phase of teacher education needs to be a shared
      responsibility, 45-46
   weaknesses in traditional approaches to clinical training of
      preservice teachers, 38
Meade (1991) describes
   specific processes for developing teacher-education internships,
      86
Megargee (1990)
   psychology internships to gain firsthand experience about
      chosen profession, 25
mentor as a master teacher, 86

mentoring and tutoring valuable for educational institution and
service learner, 66
mentor/protege model, 44
Michigan State University, 50
Middlesex County College in New Jersey
collaborative agreement with Ford Motor Co., 52
minority teacher candidates
arrangements to recruit into teacher education programs, 54
Model U.N. program, 25
Moore (1990)
discussion of Kolb's theory by, 7
Moore (1994a)
discusses the changing images of work and impact on college-
level instruction, 10
Moore (1994b)
implications of a changing workplace for experiential education,
12
more workers will need retraining, 67
Mosier (1990)
experiential educational activities benefits from a college
president's perspective, 69
more workers will need retraining, 67
Mosser (1989)
cognitive development outcomes, 23
goals of a liberal-arts education, 19
goals should be necessary parts of all college liberal-arts
programs, 21
outcome indicators, 32
Mosser and Rea (1990)
marketing experiential education programs to minority or
nontraditional students, 16
motivation as key to learning, 8
Muldoon and Myrick (1995)
Model U.N. program of, 25
Muller (1989)
costs of supervising students off-campus or at the work site, 16
discussed justification of faculty time for supervision of
interns, 83

N

National Alliance of Business
examples for higher education participation, 74

National Archives
  cooperative-education internship venture with, 31
National Board for Professional Teaching Standards, 38
National Commission for Cooperative Education, 2
National Service Corps, 11
Neapolitan (1992)
  value of internships, 71
need for broader understanding of the purposes of education and
      best ways to teach, 26
Newmann (1990)
  "an agenda for reflection" of, 58
New York State Senate Minority Summer Interim Program, 27
New York University, 75-76
      AmeriCorps-Steward Park High School partnership, 76
nontraditional learners with multitude of learning styles and needs
    as issue that needs to be addressed, 8
Northeastern University, 38
Northfield (1989)
      practicum and seminar courses to ensure proper reflection about
        experiences, 85
Novak (1989)
      cooperative-education internship venture with National
        Archives, 31
      relationships with the National Archives on learning in
        communication arts, 86

O

O'Brien (1993)
    study of college students' employment activities, 50
"Observer-Project" at Lehman College in the Bronx, 63
off-campus and full-time internships, 72
Office of Experiential Education at University of Kentucky, 65
Olszewski and Bussler (1993)
    university's goal should include development of sense of social
        responsibility, 59
Oludaja (1993)
    experiential approach to teaching of intercultural
        communication, 27
O'Neil (1990)
    concerns for delivering a liberal civic education, 60
O'Neill (1992)
    students go into graduate school at increased rate after
        experiential learning, 10

Oregon State University
 student-run advertising/public-relations agency at, 30
outcome indicators for liberal-arts program, 32

P

Parker and Keeling (1990)
 marketing experiential education programs to minority or
 nontraditional students, 16
 need to market experiential learning programs, 89
Parnell (1996)
 dichotomy between sound instructional practices and
 happenings in the classroom, 6
Participatory Design
 involvement of worker in management of work flow and
 organization, 12
partnerships as a most necessary for successful work-study
 arrangements, 54
PATC. See Professional Automotive Training Center
Paull et al. (1995)
 description of efforts to restructure a program in teacher
 education, 43
Paulter (1991)
 framework for clinical experience development based upon five
 goals, 43
 specific processes for developing teacher-education internships,
 86
 three-level program plan, 43
Pepperdine University, 43
performance objectives
 need in order to guide experiential learning activity, 90
 use in health-career areas, 87
physics
 value of experiential learning in teaching of introductory, 49
pitfalls in the field experience that should be addressed by teacher
 educators, 55
Polirstok (1996)
 sees connection between learning environment and student
 cultural experiences, 9
political aspects of college institutional curriculum decision making
 need to consider, 82
Portwood and Naish (1993)
 need for business-college linkages for professional workforce
 education, 50

four criteria necessary for, 39
regularly scheduled class provides hands-on experience, 85
Reynolds (1942)
    fieldwork experience helps a student develop a "professional
        attitude", 48-49
Rheams and Saint (1991)
    describe successful program designs for experiential learning
        activities, 87
    ongoing changes require different methods of educating
        workers, 70
Roebuck and Hochman (1993)
    description of partnership of teacher education and community
        service agencies, 46
roles required to make experiential learning successful and
        workable, 35
Rosenbaum et al. (1992)
    movement to apprenticeship as experiential learning for
        structured workforce, 52
Russell (1993)
    professional teacher preparation requires "reflection-in-action",
        41
    weaknesses in traditional approaches to clinical training of
        preservice teachers, 38

S
sabbaticals of faculty
    importance of, 73
Sault Saint Marie Michigan businesses, 50
Schmitigal (1993)
    encourages students to provide service to firm in their rural
        community, 78
    study of business communications students engaged in
        collaborative project, 50
school administrator preparation program, 45
School to Work Opportunities Act of 1994, 74-75
sciences and engineering
    business perspective of experiential learning in the, 49
Seibert and Davenport-Sypher (1989)
    college retention rates improved as a result of experiential
        learning involvement, 9
    document the benefits of experiential learning for student career
        decision making, 10
Sellnow (1992) discuss

internships which provided opportunities for, 87
social work training
    objectives of fieldwork training, 48
Soter (1993)
        concern with worker training and educational - business
        relationships, 51
Spiritual Growth
    need for total-quality relationships, 12
Stanton (1990a)
    experiential learning pedagogy and the liberal arts not mutually
        exclusive, 19
Stanton (1990b, 1988) definition of service learning, 57
State Center Community College District, 54
Stone and Wonser (1990)
    students learn "when they regard what they need to know as
        relevant...", 26
Stross (1995) describes primary care preceptorship through
        contextual learning, 47
student-active methods of learning
    as largely self-directed, 31
student-run radio stations
    Thompsen (1991) description of effort aimed at creating realistic,
        32
student selection for external experiential learning
    methods for, 84
students should not receive compensation for learning experiences,
        90
students tend to continue their education into graduate school
    at significantly increased rate after experiential learning, 10
student volunteerism benefit for faculty, 70
successful program designs for experiential learning activities, 87-
        88
SUNY Buffalo
    educational administration program at, 45
Swearer Center for Public Service approach, 61

T
Taylor and Samaras (1994)
    weaknesses in traditional approaches to clinical training of
        preservice teachers, 38
Taylor (1990) describes
    specific processes for developing teacher-education internships,
        86

teacher induction partnership program at, 43-44

University of Tennessee at Knoxville, 39-40

university's goal should include development of sense of social
        responsibility, 59

"user friendly" ways to make experiential education more, 71

V

Valli and Taylor (1987)
    thoughts on curriculum of, 39

Virginia Community College Sysem in Richmond, ix

Voge, Susan, xi

W

Waddell (1991) suggests strengthens programs
    recruitment of at-risk students, 84

Wade (1994)
    mentoring and tutoring valuable for educational institution and
        service learner, 66

Wagner et al. (1992)
    factors that complicate experiential learning activities, 15

Wagner, Scharinger, and Sisak (1995),
    factors that complicate experiential learning activities, 15

Walter (1994)
    School to Work Opportunities Act of 1994, 74-75

Washington (1992)
    benefits and issues of experiential learning in professional
        preparation programs, 47

Washington Center for Internships, 88-89

Wattson (1992)
    experiential learning as a process to ensure integration of such
        values, 22
    regularly scheduled class provides hands-on experience, 85

Weinmann (1992)
    Mosser's goals should be necessary parts of all college liberal-
        arts programs, 21

West Georgia College (1989), 31

Workforce 2000 Report, 67
    majority of all new employment will require higher education,
        70

Worthington (1992)
    small-business institute as a means to bring real world to
        advertising program, 70

Y

Z

ASHE-ERIC HIGHER EDUCATION REPORTS

Since 1983, the Association for the Study of Higher Education (ASHE) and the Educational Resources Information Center (ERIC) Clearinghouse on Higher Education, a sponsored project of the Graduate School of Education and Human Development at The George Washington University, have cosponsored the ASHE-ERIC Higher Education Report series. The 1995 series is the twenty-fourth overall and the seventh to be published by the Graduate School of Education and Human Development at The George Washington University.

Each monograph is the definitive analysis of a tough higher education problem, based on thorough research of pertinent literature and institutional experiences. Topics are identified by a national survey. Noted practitioners and scholars are then commissioned to write the reports, with experts providing critical reviews of each manuscript before publication.

Eight monographs (10 before 1985) in the ASHE-ERIC Higher Education Report series are published each year and are available on individual and subscription bases. To order, use the order form on the last page of this book.

Qualified persons interested in writing a monograph for the ASHE-ERIC Higher Education Report series are invited to submit a proposal to the National Advisory Board. As the preeminent literature review and issue analysis series in higher education, the Higher Education Reports are guaranteed wide dissemination and national exposure for accepted candidates. Execution of a monograph requires at least a minimal familiarity with the ERIC database, including *Resources in Education* and the current *Index to Journals in Education*. The objective of these reports is to bridge conventional wisdom with practical research. Prospective authors are strongly encouraged to call Dr. Fife at 800-773-3742.

For further information, write to
    ASHE-ERIC Higher Education Reports
    The George Washington University
    One Dupont Circle, Suite 630
    Washington, DC 20036
Or phone (202) 296-2597; toll free: 800-773-ERIC.

Write or call for a complete catalog.

ADVISORY BOARD

James Earl Davis
University of Delaware at Newark

Susan Frost
Emory University

Mildred Garcia
Montclair State College

James Hearn
University of Georgia

Bruce Anthony Jones
University of Pittsburgh

L. Jackson Newell
Deep Springs College

Carolyn Thompson
State University of New York–Buffalo

CONSULTING EDITORS

Keith Miser
Colorado State University

Diane E. Morrison
Centre for Curriculum and Professional Development

L. Jackson Newell
University of Utah

Steven G. Olswang
University of Washington

Sherry Sayles-Folks
Eastern Michigan University

Karl Schilling
Miami University

Charles Schroeder
University of Missouri

Lawrence A. Sherr
University of Kansas

Marilla D. Svinicki
University of Texas at Austin

Kathe Taylor
State of Washington Higher Education Coordinating Board

Donald H. Wulff
University of Washington

REVIEW PANEL

Charles Adams
University of Massachusetts–Amherst

Louis Albert
American Association for Higher Education

Richard Alfred
University of Michigan

Henry Lee Allen
University of Rochester

Philip G. Altbach
Boston College

Marilyn J. Amey
University of Kansas

Kristine L. Anderson
Florida Atlantic University

Karen D. Arnold
Boston College

Robert J. Barak
Iowa State Board of Regents

Alan Bayer
Virginia Polytechnic Institute and State University

John P. Bean
Indiana University–Bloomington

John M. Braxton
Peabody College, Vanderbilt University

Ellen M. Brier
Tennessee State University

Barbara E. Brittingham
The University of Rhode Island

Dennis Brown
University of Kansas

Peter McE. Buchanan
Council for Advancement and Support of Education

Patricia Carter
University of Michigan

John A. Centra
Syracuse University

Arthur W. Chickering
George Mason University

Darrel A. Clowes
Virginia Polytechnic Institute and State University

Cynthia S. Dickens
Mississippi State University

Deborah M. DiCroce
Piedmont Virginia Community College

Sarah M. Dinham
University of Arizona

Kenneth A. Feldman
State University of New York–Stony Brook

Dorothy E. Finnegan
The College of William & Mary

Mildred Garcia
Montclair State College

Rodolfo Z. Garcia
Commission on Institutions of Higher Education

Kenneth C. Green
University of Southern California

James Hearn
University of Georgia

Edward R. Hines
Illinois State University

Deborah Hunter
University of Vermont

Philo Hutcheson
Georgia State University

Bruce Anthony Jones
University of Pittsburgh

Elizabeth A. Jones
The Pennsylvania State University

Kathryn Kretschmer
University of Kansas

Marsha V. Krotseng
State College and University Systems of West Virginia

George D. Kuh
Indiana University–Bloomington

Daniel T. Layzell
University of Wisconsin System

Patrick G. Love
Kent State University

Cheryl D. Lovell
State Higher Education Executive Officers

Meredith Jane Ludwig
American Association of State Colleges and Universities

Dewayne Matthews
Western Interstate Commission for Higher Education

Mantha V. Mehallis
Florida Atlantic University

Toby Milton
Essex Community College

James R. Mingle
State Higher Education Executive Officers

John A. Muffo
Virginia Polytechnic Institute and State University

L. Jackson Newell
Deep Springs College

James C. Palmer
Illinois State University

Robert A. Rhoads
The Pennsylvania State University

G. Jeremiah Ryan
Harford Community College

Mary Ann Danowitz Sagaria
The Ohio State University

Daryl G. Smith
The Claremont Graduate School

William G. Tierney
University of Southern California

Susan B. Twombly
University of Kansas

Robert A. Walhaus
University of Illinois–Chicago

Harold Wechsler
University of Rochester

Elizabeth J. Whitt
University of Illinois–Chicago

Michael J. Worth
The George Washington University

RECENT TITLES

1995 ASHE-ERIC Higher Education Reports

1. Tenure, Promotion, and Reappointment: Legal and Administrative Implications
   Benjamin Baez and John A. Centra

2. Taking Teaching Seriously: Meeting the Challenge of Instructional Improvement
   Michael B. Paulsen and Kenneth A. Feldman

3. Empowering the Faculty: Mentoring Redirected and Renewed
   Gaye Luna and Deborah L. Cullen

4. Enhancing Student Learning: Intellectual, Social, and Emotional Integration
   Anne Goodsell Love and Patrick G. Love

5. Benchmarking in Higher Education: Adapting Best Practices to Improve Quality
   Jeffrey W. Alstete

6. Models for Improving College Teaching: A Faculty Resource
   Jon E. Travis

1994 ASHE-ERIC Higher Education Reports

1. The Advisory Committee Advantage: Creating an Effective Strategy for Programmatic Improvement
   Lee Teitel

2. Collaborative Peer Review: The Role of Faculty in Improving College Teaching
   Larry Keig and Michael D. Waggoner

3. Prices, Productivity, and Investment: Assessing Financial Strategies in Higher Education
   Edward P. St. John

4. The Development Officer in Higher Education: Toward an Understanding of the Role
   Michael J. Worth and James W. Asp II

5. The Promises and Pitfalls of Performance Indicators in Higher Education
   Gerald Gaither, Brian P. Nedwek, and John E. Neal

6. A New Alliance: Continuous Quality and Classroom Effectiveness
   Mimi Wolverton

7. Redesigning Higher Education: Producing Dramatic Gains in Student Learning
   Lion F. Gardiner

8. Student Learning outside the Classroom: Transcending Artificial Boundaries
   George D. Kuh, Katie Branch Douglas, Jon P. Lund, and Jackie Ramin-Gyurnek

1993 ASHE-ERIC Higher Education Reports

1. The Department Chair: New Roles, Responsibilities, and Challenges
   Alan T. Seagren, John W. Creswell, and Daniel W. Wheeler

2. Sexual Harassment in Higher Education: From Conflict to Community
   Robert O. Riggs, Patricia H. Murrell, and Joann C. Cutting

3. Chicanos in Higher Education: Issues and Dilemmas for the 21st Century
   Adalberto Aguirre, Jr., and Ruben O. Martinez

4. Academic Freedom in American Higher Education: Rights, Responsibilities, and Limitations
   Robert K. Poch

5. Making Sense of the Dollars: The Costs and Uses of Faculty Compensation
   Kathryn M. Moore and Marilyn J. Amey

6. Enhancing Promotion, Tenure, and Beyond: Faculty Socialization as a Cultural Process
   William C. Tierney and Robert A. Rhoads

7. New Perspectives for Student Affairs Professionals: Evolving Realities, Responsibilities, and Roles
   Peter H. Garland and Thomas W. Grace

8. Turning Teaching into Learning: The Role of Student Responsibility in the Collegiate Experience
   Todd M. Davis and Patricia Hillman Murrell

1992 ASHE-ERIC Higher Education Reports

1. The Leadership Compass: Values and Ethics in Higher Education
   John R. Wilcox and Susan L. Ebbs

2. Preparing for a Global Community: Achieving an International Perspective in Higher Education
   Sarah M. Pickert

3. Quality: Transforming Postsecondary Education
   Ellen Earle Chaffee and Lawrence A. Sherr

4. Faculty Job Satisfaction: Women and Minorities in Peril
   Martha Wingard Tack and Carol Logan Patitu

5. Reconciling Rights and Responsibilities of Colleges and Students: Offensive Speech, Assembly, Drug Testing, and Safety
   Annette Gibbs

6. Creating Distinctiveness: Lessons from Uncommon Colleges and Universities
   Barbara K. Townsend, L. Jackson Newell, and Michael D. Wiese

7. Instituting Enduring Innovations: Achieving Continuity of Change in Higher Education
   Barbara K. Curry

8. Crossing Pedagogical Oceans: International Teaching Assistants in U.S. Undergraduate Education
   Rosslyn M. Smith, Patricia Byrd, Gayle L. Nelson, Ralph Pat Barrett, and Janet C. Constantinides

1991 ASHE-ERIC Higher Education Reports

1. Active Learning: Creating Excitement in the Classroom
   Charles C. Bonwell and James A. Eison

2. Realizing Gender Equality in Higher Education: The Need to Integrate Work/Family Issues
   Nancy Hensel

3. Academic Advising for Student Success: A System of Shared Responsibility
   Susan H. Frost

4. Cooperative Learning: Increasing College Faculty Instructional Productivity
   David W. Johnson, Roger T. Johnson, and Karl A. Smith

5. High School–College Partnerships: Conceptual Models, Programs, and Issues
   Arthur Richard Greenberg

6. Meeting the Mandate: Renewing the College and Departmental Curriculum
   William Toombs and William Tierney

7. Faculty Collaboration: Enhancing the Quality of Scholarship and Teaching
   Ann E. Austin and Roger G. Baldwin

8. Strategies and Consequences: Managing the Costs in Higher Education
   John S. Waggaman